fast family food

To my darling daughter Nini,
forever my inspiration, my love,
my best friend.

Rebecca Wilson
fast family food

contents

slow cooker

no cook

hello and welcome
to fast family food!

If you're picking this book up, it means you're a fan of good, honest, wholesome grub. The type of food that's really easy to put together and everyone wants seconds of. Whether you have a child at weaning age, fussy older children to cater for or it's just you adults at home, this book is for you.

Forget the stress of long, complicated recipes, which require you to stand at the stove and stir for ages. Every dish in this book can be prepped in 10 minutes or less. Start cooking with a quick initial burst of activity, then before you know it the food will either be done and ready to eat or you can allow the hob, oven or slow cooker to do its thing while you relax... or, let's face it, get on with some other jobs on the to-do list!

It'll make your life easier if you know what you're doing before you start, so read the recipe through first and get the required pots and pans out. Find all the ingredients on the list and get them ready on the counter. Check whether the oven or grill wants preheating and put the kettle on if boiling water is needed. Crucially, set the kids up with an activity so you at least have a chance of cracking on uninterrupted (you can find a few of my favourite tips on keeping the little ones entertained on page 19).

The 10-minute prep time will be a cinch on some recipes, but others may require a little more focus and speed. However, if you prefer to be a little more leisurely in the kitchen, or you do get interrupted by the little ones, don't worry about it taking a little longer. Cooking should always be done at your own pace.

Some recipes in this book have been photographed with a few extra side dishes – these are completely optional and just there to give you an idea of how you might want to adapt the meal to suit the individual needs and tastes of your own family.

I hope you and your family love these recipes as much as mine do! I love to see your handiwork, so tag me on Instagram at @rebeccawilsonfood with all your delicious creations!

Rebecca
X

cooking for all the family

WHY SHOULD WE EAT WITH OUR BABIES AND CHILDREN?

Studies show that eating with your children helps to raise confident little eaters. Our little ones watch us and naturally want to copy what we do, so by showing them how much we enjoy a variety of healthy foods, we can encourage them to be a little more open to trying new tastes and textures. The hope is that as they grow older, fussy tendencies will be minimized by us leading with a positive eating example. Not only this, but modelling how you physically chew, swallow, eat, drink and use cutlery is invaluable for helping your baby learn how to do it themselves. And the best bit – you only need to cook once, making feeding your family that much easier!

HOW TO CUT AND SERVE THE FOOD IN THIS BOOK

To make the meals we cook suitable for the tiniest of taste testers, we need to cut and serve the food in an appropriate way. The aim is to make it easy for little ones to hold the food and feed themselves, so cutting foods into finger-sized strips where possible is ideal. Items that come in a round patty shape, like a small pancake which babies can easily hold themselves, can be left whole. The idea is to encourage little ones to independently enjoy eating in the safest way possible. Food that babies can take bites of is usually safer for them to eat than food that's cut into bite-sized pieces, as they are determining how much they can handle, which reduces the risk of choking. There are some exceptions to this rule – whole foods which must be cut into a smaller size to be safe to serve to little ones. Grapes, for instance, must be at least halved lengthways (I usually go for quartered for peace of mind). As a general rule, if the food is a round shape approx. 1–4cm ($^1/_2$–$1^1/_2$in) in diameter, then this should be cut into a smaller size, and ideally into long thin pieces rather than wide pieces. Any foods larger than this generally can be served whole or cut into finger strips. However, there's no need to get the ruler out, this is just an example if you're seeking more specific guidance. It's always good to play it by

ear and trust our instinct when it comes to feeding our kids. Here's a few examples of first foods and how to serve them:

Citrus fruits Peel the whole fruit and cut it in half widthways, keeping the segments attached. Baby will be able to pick up the whole fruit and eat from the cut side, which will mash easily in their mouth.

Bananas Separate into strips by pushing your finger down the centre of a peeled banana, it will naturally divide into 3 long strips which aren't slimy and are perfect for baby to hold.

Toast Lightly butter or top toast with some mashed fruit or yogurt to soften it a little, then cut into finger-sized strips.

Hard-boiled eggs Peel and cut into quarters, lengthways.

Peas, sweetcorn kernels and pomegranate seeds These can be served whole as they are too small to be a choking hazard. Corn on the cob can be served cut into 5cm (2in) rounds so it's easy for little ones to pick up.

CHOKING VS GAGGING

Some parents worry a lot about the risk of choking when serving solid food to their little one for the first time, especially with finger foods. It's something to be taken seriously, however, let me reassure you that it is rare for babies to choke. Therefore, it is equally important to avoid letting this worry stop you from serving a wide variety of foods to your baby. By holding back from offering finger foods, you may unintentionally restrict their diet or avoid allowing them to develop their eating skills. Note that studies have shown there is no greater risk of choking when offering finger foods to baby vs just purées. Nonetheless, it is still important to be vigilant, just in case. I recommend taking a first aid course if you can, or researching baby CPR before you start weaning so you feel confident that you'd know what to do in a worst-case scenario. Here are a few steps you can also take to lessen the risk:

- Do not leave baby alone when eating.

- Make sure they're in an upright seated position, ideally in a high chair and not on your lap.

- Ensure baby is developmentally ready to start eating (see page 11).

- Always serve food in a safe way – see foods to avoid (page 10).

- Avoid serving food in walkers or bouncers, as the sudden movements can be dangerous.

When you begin to offer solid foods to baby, they're likely to experience gagging in those first few months. Gagging is very different to choking, it's a completely normal reflex that happens as baby gets used to solid food being in certain places in their mouth. Gagging will be noisy, as baby will be visibly trying to change the location of the food, bringing it forwards from the back of their mouth. You will know it is gagging if baby is coughing and making grunting or retching noises, and can still be seen to be breathing. Intervention is not needed for gagging, and it can often be more dangerous if you try to remove the food yourself, as you might accidentally push it further in. Remain vigilant and ready to help if choking begins, but allow baby to fix the gagging problem themselves. It is a normal part of your little one learning how to eat – however difficult it might be for us adults to watch.

Choking, on the other hand, is when an object is lodged in baby's throat and blocking their airways, and this must be acted on immediately by the care giver. If they are choking, baby will be making very little noise (in contrast to gagging). They will either not be breathing or struggling to take breaths, which will be visible by the chest and ribs being pulled in. In this instance, quickly remove baby from their high chair, then lean them forward, supporting their chin and chest as needed, and give five firm pats on the back between their shoulder blades with the heel of your hand. Continue to follow the baby CPR process. This aspect of weaning may seem scary, but understanding the risks and what you might need to do if needed is really just a safety precaution, so try not to let any worry take the fun and joy out of feeding your family.

Got no teeth? It is a common misconception that babies need teeth to eat finger foods. In fact, their gums are hard enough to chew and break down food from the age of 6 months. Some babies do not grow their first teeth until they are over a year old, and in most cases the back molars (chewing teeth) usually don't come in until 18 months plus, which is too long to wait to serve finger foods.

SALT AND SUGAR
Every recipe in this book can be served to every member of your family, including babies aged 6 months and up. The recipes have been specifically developed to be low in salt and sugar so that they are safe for little ones to enjoy but still delicious for us adults too (some recipes, such as the Strawberry Pop Tarts on page 67, include specific instructions where moderation for babies is advised). However, not everyone has the same preference when it comes to seasoning – it's something we learn to get a taste for as we get older. Therefore, please do feel free to season your own food to your taste once the family meal has been dished up, or when your little one's portion has been removed from the pan. Adapt these recipes with extra chilli, pepper, sugar or spice if you feel like it too. Really make it your own – because food is there to be enjoyed!

Salt intake guide

- Babies under 12 months should have less than 1g salt per day (0.4g sodium)

- Toddlers aged 1–3 years should have a maximum of 2g salt per day (0.8g sodium)

- Children aged 4–6 years should have a maximum of 3g salt per day (1.2g sodium)

- Children aged 7–10 years should have a maximum of 5g salt per day (2g sodium)

- Children aged 11 years plus and adults should have a maximum of 6g salt per day (2.4g sodium)

FOODS TO AVOID FOR LITTLE ONES

Saturated Fat Be mindful to limit your child's intake of saturated fat in foods like cakes, biscuits and cookies and crisps (potato chips). Babies and young children need lots of healthy fats in their diets, found in foods like avocado and milk, as they are using lots of energy growing, learning and being active, so choose full-fat versions of dairy products like milk or cheese.

Sugar Try to avoid too many sugary treats for little ones, as over-exposure to sweet tastes can lead to a preference for sugary flavours. This also includes naturally occurring sugars in foods like fresh fruit juices, as it can lead to tooth decay. I have developed these recipes to be lower in sugar, and using sugar derived from more natural sources like maple syrup, and sugar naturally occurring in fruit. If a recipe requires a fruit purée pouch, this is simply an unsweetened 100% fruit baby purée pouch found in the baby food aisle. Be sure to use one which has no added cereals, and try to opt for a sweet flavour like apple purée or mango purée – no problem if it's a mix of a few different fruits.

Honey Honey can contain bacteria that can produce toxins in baby's intestines leading to infant botulism, which is a very serious illness. Avoid serving honey to babies under the age of 12 months. This includes shop-bought products that contain honey in the ingredients, so always read the packaging.

Raw eggs From 6 months, you can serve eggs to baby. In the UK, choose hen's eggs that have the British Lion quality stamp on them, which are safe to serve raw as an ingredient in food like homemade mayonnaise, or lightly cooked like a soft-boiled egg. If the eggs are not British Lion stamped or you are in doubt, always fully cook the white and yolk of the egg until they are solid before serving to baby. This also includes duck, goose or quail's eggs.

Soy sauce This is normally very high in salt and so is not recommended for use in baby or toddler foods. Instead, choosing a low-salt soy sauce can be a good swap for the whole family – but be careful as each brand is different, with some still containing too much salt. Try to choose a low-salt variety that has less than 6g per 100ml of salt on the label.

Whole nuts Avoid serving whole nuts and peanuts to babies and children under the age of 5 years as they are a choking hazard. Nut butters, crushed nuts and ground nuts can be served to baby from around the age of 6 months.

Certain cheeses Cheese is packed full of calcium, protein and vitamins, making it a fantastic food to serve to babies and young children as part of a varied diet. However, it is advised to offer only pasteurized full-fat cheese from the age of 6 months. This includes hard cheese, like Cheddar, cottage cheese and soft cream cheese.

There is a risk of the bacteria listeria in soft cheese like Brie, Camembert, ripened goat's cheese, blue cheese or cheese made from unpasteurized milk. Listeria can make baby feel very ill so it's best to avoid. However, you can use these cheeses to cook with, as the listeria is killed during cooking.

Rice drinks Babies and young children up to the age of 5 years, should not drink rice-based drinks – especially not as a replacement for breast milk or formula milk – as they contain high levels of arsenic. Babies are fine to eat rice as the levels are monitored in the EU for rice and rice products.

Raw shellfish Always fully cook shellfish such as mussels, oysters, clams and cockles to avoid the risk of food poisoning.

Shark, swordfish and marlin Avoid shark, swordfish and marlin as the high levels of mercury found in these fish can affect the development of baby's nervous system.

Garlic-infused oil A small handful of countries advise against using garlic-infused oil when cooking for children under 12 months. This usually applies to home-made varieties. If you prefer to avoid, swap like-for-like quantities with a flavourless cooking oil like sunflower oil.

Self-rising flour Unlike self-raising flour in the UK, self-rising flour in the US usually has added salt. You can make your own to keep salt levels down by adding 1 tsp of baking powder per each 150g (1 cup) of plain (all-purpose) flour.

weaning advice

Every recipe in this book is suitable for all ages, from 6-month-old babies to older siblings and us adults. Therefore, you can wean your baby using the recipes in this book. Before you get started, let me answer some of the most common questions I get asked about offering first foods to baby.

What equipment do I need? There isn't a huge list of items you'll need, but here are some useful things you could start to collect as your baby is coming up to weaning age.

- A straight-back high chair with a safety harness. This should either come with a tray, or you should be able to attach it or position it very close to the family dinner table. Never leave baby unattended in the high chair when they are eating. If the high chair has shoulder straps, ensure they aren't so tight that baby is held back and can't lean forwards – if baby was to gag on a piece of food, we want them to be able to lean forwards to help dislodge it themselves.

- Use soft weaning utensils at first, which are kinder on baby's gums than metal spoons. As you progress with weaning, you can offer baby a soft-grip metal toddler spoon and fork to help them start learning how to use cutlery.

- A good silicone catcher bib and/or a long-sleeved bib. I always liked to layer these two up with the long-sleeved bib underneath to save baby's clothes, and the catcher bib on top to minimize food waste.

- A small open cup or a valve-free sippy cup for water with meals. It's a good idea to allow baby to practise their drinking from the beginning of weaning so they have plenty of time to master this useful skill. Babies under 12 months don't actually need the extra hydration, their breast milk or formula milk will be enough, but it helps to start learning early.

- A small, child-friendly bowl and plate, preferably with good suction underneath to attach it to the table and ultimately minimize food waste.

- Reusable storage boxes, non-stick baking paper and/or foil to store leftovers and batch cooking.

How do I know when my baby is ready for solid food? There are a few factors to consider when assessing whether your baby is ready for solid food. Common misconceptions, things that people often put down to baby being ready for solid foods, include them waking more in the night, chewing on fists, watching you eat intently or wanting extra milk feeds. However, these are usually just signs of teething or developmental traits, which are normal behavioural milestones that often occur around the same age. These signs alone are not enough to tell you that baby is ready to eat. Instead look out for the following:

- Baby will be around 6 months old, as this is generally when their body has developed enough to digest and process solid food.

- Baby will be able to coordinate their own eyes, hands and mouth to see food, pick it up and bring it to their mouth.

- Baby will be able to stay in an upright sitting position for at least one minute, without leaning on you or another object – this is important to minimize the risk of choking. They should also have good stability in their neck and be able to hold their head up with ease.

- Baby's tongue thrust reflex has lessened and they will be able to swallow food, rather than automatically spit it out. If baby pushes their tongue forward naturally and spits out all their food, wait a couple of days and try again, this reflex will go soon.

Should I do baby-led weaning or spoon feeding?
Firstly, let me explain what the difference is.
Baby-led weaning, or simply 'finger foods', as I like
to call them, is when you offer your baby whole solid
foods to independently pick up and feed themselves.
Finger foods help little ones to learn the skill of eating
at a quicker pace. This method also introduces baby
to a wider variety of foods, visually, texturally and
in terms of flavour, which in turn can lead to a
confident eater and hopefully minimize fussiness.

Spoon feeding, on the other hand, is where you
blend baby's meals into a purée with a little milk
or water (you can make a purée using any of the
recipes in this book, so you're still able to eat together
as a family) and feed baby the purée using a spoon.
The reason people often spoon feed to start with,
is that it may feel a more manageable and familiar
process to both baby and parent. If you decide
to take this route, it's important to note that the
consistency of baby's purée should evolve from
smooth to slightly textured within the first couple
of days–weeks of weaning. Go at a pace you feel
comfortable with, bearing in mind that the end
goal is to be serving coarse/lumpy purées, followed
by roughly mashed textures by the time baby is
10–11 months old, ready for them to transition to
finger foods around their first birthday.

My favourite approach is to use a combination
of both baby-led weaning and spoon feeding.
From the age of 6 months, I like to offer baby a few
pieces of finger food alongside a puréed version of
the same food. I'd recommend doing this for the first
2–6 weeks to ease baby into eating solid food and
allow them to taste the same flavour in a variety
of ways. Remember that the goal of weaning is to
teach baby how to eat, not to feed them until they
are full up, as before the age of 12 months they will
still get most of their nutrition from breast milk or
formula milk. For this reason, try not to worry too
much about the amount of food baby is eating at the
start. Weaning is all about learning the physical skill
of eating and getting baby used to a wide variety
of foods, so that when they do need to rely on solid
food for their main nutrition, they have the ability
and the desire to eat a healthy balanced diet.

How to start? For the first 1–2 weeks, it's best to
ease baby into solid foods starting with soft steamed
and/or puréed vegetables to ensure they won't
develop a preference for sweet foods early on. Up
until 6 months, baby has only ever experienced their
comforting, sweet-tasting milk, so it will be helpful in
the long run to get baby used to the fact that solid
food tastes different to this familiar sweetness.
You may experience a few funny faces or unsure
responses, but this doesn't mean that baby doesn't
like it, it simply tells us that it's new and they are
trying to figure it all out.

It's important that we don't presume baby doesn't
like new flavours, then avoid serving them again,
as we would be unintentionally restricting their diet
by making it harder for baby to learn to love that
food in the long run. This same logic applies when
toddlers and slightly older children refuse certain
foods – keep offering on a regular basis, as it can
take up to 20 times of offering a food for little one
to learn to love it.

How to cook vegetables for baby's first tastes
Steaming helps lock in all the nutrients and is the
healthiest way to cook vegetables for newly weaning
babies. This veg can be the same as what you are
having with your meal, so you're only cooking once
and baby can learn by watching you eat.

To steam vegetables, half-fill a medium-large
saucepan with boiling water from the kettle and
place over a high heat. Use a steamer attachment
with a lid, or create a make-shift steamer by placing
a metal colander over the pan with a large lid on
top. Wash and peel the raw veg, if necessary, then
cut it into the appropriate size and shape for baby
– it simply needs to be an easy shape for baby to
pick up independently. For newly weaning babies,
steam until the veg is soft enough to squish between
your fingers. Now you can either serve as is for
baby-led weaning, or mash using a fork, or potato
masher or whizz in a blender if serving to baby on
a spoon. Here are a few examples to help if you're
unsure on how to get started with finger foods, but
there's no need to get the ruler out as this is just a
rough guide:

- Root vegetables like carrots and parsnips – cut into approx. 2cm (³/₄in) wide and 7cm (2³/₄in) long batons and steam for 12–15 minutes.

- Courgette (zucchini) – cut into batons (the same size as for root veg) and steam for around 6 minutes.

- Broccoli – cut into medium-sized florets and steam for around 6 minutes.

- Green beans – remove woody ends and steam for around 7 minutes.

Once you have served a good variety of veggies, move on to offering soft fruits like bananas, soft nectarine wedges, quartered strawberries, etc. After a week or two of baby trying lots of veggies and fruits, if you feel confident enough you can move on to the next stage of weaning by offering the recipes within this book. It may seem daunting at first, but don't worry – they will be able to handle much more than you expect. Their gums are hard enough to break down most soft foods, so it doesn't matter if they've not got any teeth yet. Ultimately, it's great to offer baby a wide variety of flavours and textures because it will help them learn how to eat quicker.

Remember, if you don't feel confident going straight into just finger foods, you can blend down the recipes in this book with some extra liquid and serve alongside some of the same food in finger food format if you wish. You'll still get all the benefits of eating together and saving so much time with cooking just once per meal.

What meal is best to start with? This really depends on the schedule you, your family and your baby have. Try to find a time when baby is happy, not too hungry, but also importantly not too full from their last milk feed. Ideally around half an hour before their next scheduled milk feed, so that you can offer milk after the feeding session is over. If you can, time it so that you eat your meal alongside baby too (see page 8).

How do I know what size portion to give baby? As adults, we have recommended portion sizes to ensure we don't over-eat. However, for babies, there are no recommended portion sizes. Every baby is different – they all learn to eat at a different pace and have different activity levels and appetites. Be mindful of your baby's wet and dirty nappies, ensure they are steadily putting on weight and, if you have any concerns, contact your health visitor or doctor.

Before the age of one, food is all about exploring different tastes and textures, as well as adding vital nutrients to baby's diet. Milk is still baby's main source of nutrition. So with that in mind, parents can relax from the worry that baby hasn't eaten enough. Focus on encouraging baby to try a variety of foods. If baby just picks it up and takes one mouthful, that's totally fine! Equally, if baby wolfs down the whole lot, that is fine too – they could be going through a growth spurt and need those extra calories.

The great thing about taking a baby-led weaning approach, is that it encourages baby to follow their own appetite. Baby is more likely to be able to recognize when they are full and stop eating – or start playing with the food!

adapting the recipes to suit your diet

If you have specific dietary requirements, whether dairy-free, gluten-free, egg-free, vegan or vegetarian, there are ways to adapt the recipes in this book to suit your family's needs. Look out for the * symbol next to the ingredients in the recipes to see which ones you can substitute. Here, I have listed some foods that you can use as substitutes – unless it is specifically stated in the recipe, choose whichever one works best for you. Always check product packets for hidden ingredients you may not be aware of.

DAIRY-FREE COOKING

Butter For most recipes, you can replace butter with dairy-free spreads (these are better for baking), or with coconut oil, olive oil or sunflower oil.

Milk You can substitute dairy milk for a plant-based alternative in all recipes. For under 2s, all milk should be full-fat to ensure little ones are taking enough energy from their food. Soy, pea and oat milks are all a suitable swap from 6 months onwards. Nut and hemp milks can be served to children over 2 years old, although do bear in mind that these are lower in calories, so not always an ideal staple for young children. Avoid rice milk in general as this is not suitable for children under the age of 5 years. Try to choose a milk that is fortified with extra vitamins to ramp up the nutritional intake.

Cheese There are many dairy-free cheeses on the market these days, shop around and find ones which you like the taste of and melt well. It is best to choose a cheese alternative that is fortified with B12 and other vitamins, if possible. Alternatively, in most recipes you can just leave out the cheese or swap it for nutritional yeast flakes (about 1 tablespoon replaces 40–50g/1½–2oz of cheese), however, be mindful that in both cases this may reduce a little of the moisture content in the finished dish.

Dairy cream, cream cheese and yogurt In most supermarkets, you will find plant-based alternatives to these products. If you do struggle to find anything, use an alternative that is a similar texture to what you are trying to replace. For example, you could replace Greek yogurt with plant-based yogurt or plant-based cream cheese thinned down with a little plant-based milk. Don't be afraid to experiment and make the recipe suit you.

EGG-FREE COOKING

If egg is the main ingredient in a recipe, for example in an omelette, it is not always possible to replace with an alternative option, and so it may be best to choose another recipe in this case. However, when egg is used to bind ingredients together, such as for pancakes, flax and chia eggs are a great substitute. Be mindful that they do not expand and rise like a hen's egg would, so the results will be a little different, however, they do work to keep the ingredients together and add a little extra moisture to the recipe. To make 1 replacement egg, follow the instructions below, before adding to your recipe.

Chia egg Stir 1 tablespoon of chia seeds with 2½ tablespoons of warm water and set aside for 5 minutes.

Flax egg Stir 1 tablespoon of ground flax seeds with 3 tablespoons of warm water and set aside for 10–15 minutes.

Egg replacers In recent years, it has become much easier to purchase egg replacers in supermarkets. Look out for either powdered versions or products in the fresh fridge aisle. These are used predominantly in baking.

Egg wash alternatives When a recipe calls for an egg wash, this is to give a little sheen to your bake, especially pastry. Use plant-based milk as a substitute (soy, almond or coconut milk works best), or aquafaba – the liquid in a can of chickpeas.

GLUTEN-FREE COOKING

Gluten is the name of a protein found in wheat and some other grains. If you lead a gluten-free diet, there are plenty of alternatives. In most cases, plain (all-purpose) or self-raising flour can be replaced in like-for-like quantities with shop-bought gluten-free variations. Also, look out for gluten-free baking powder, soy sauce, Worcestershire sauce, mustard and stock cubes, as some of these products may contain traces of gluten. While oats don't contain gluten, they are often processed in factories with other grains that do, so always look for oats marked as 'gluten-free' to avoid any cross contamination.

MEAT REPLACEMENT IN RECIPES

Veggies You can generally replace meat with either firm vegetables like mushrooms or butternut squash, or meat-replacement products. Just be mindful that meat-replacement products often contain added salt, so factor this in when serving to little ones. They are also usually low in fat, therefore, it is important to replace this lost fat with other forms of higher calorific foods like avocado or nut butters, especially when serving to babies, as little ones need those extra calories to help them grow.

Tofu This is an excellent meat replacement. Use the correct firmness and follow the instructions on the packet to incorporate it into the recipe. Soft silken tofu is a good substitute for thick cream in desserts or to add at the end of cooking soups, while firm tofu is great to breadcrumb to turn into nuggets or stir through pasta or noodle dishes.

Be mindful that there are hidden traces of meat and fish in some foods like Worcestershire sauce, which usually contains anchovies, so try to find vegetarian options or leave these ingredients out. Some cheeses use animal rennet in their production, however, there are plenty on the market that are vegetarian, and this will be displayed on the packet.

NUT-FREE COOKING

When a recipe calls for peanut butter or crushed nuts, there are options you can take depending on your specific allergies. If possible, opt to substitute for nut-free butters like tahini (sesame seed paste), sunflower, or specific nut-free butters, which now exist on the market. You could also leave out the nuts altogether, however, please note that nut butters might be added as a binder or for extra moisture, so the end result may differ slightly.

A NOTE ON VANILLA EXTRACT

Traditionally, vanilla extract is made using alcohol, which you might not feel comfortable offering to little ones in its raw form. If you are adding vanilla extract to a recipe that will be cooked or baked, the quantity that ends up in the final dish is so small that all traces of alcohol will be removed in the cooking process. These days, you can buy alcohol-free vanilla extract, and this is particularly useful for no-cook recipes or if your dietary requirements don't allow any alcohol. Avoid using vanilla essence (instead of extract), as this is essentially synthetic vanilla and not ideal for little ones.

DIETARY REQUIREMENTS

GF Gluten free

V Vegetarian

EF Egg free

Vg Vegan

DF Dairy free

Look out for these icons accompanying each recipe to find out if it suits your dietary requirements. Whenever you see a * next to the letters in the dietary icon, this indicates that the recipe can be adapted to suit this dietary requirement. Please take care and turn to this section for possible alternatives to the ingredients listed.

DISCLAIMER

Those following strict allergen diets should always check the packet for guidance about suitability.

storage and freezing advice

Throughout this book, you'll find tips for loving your leftovers. Here's a few extra guidelines to help take any confusion out of how to store your food.

STORAGE AND FREEZING GUIDELINES
Although storing and freezing food is helpful when feeding your family, particularly if you're on tight schedules, it is important to do so safely, especially when feeding little tummies. All the recipes in this book that have a 'Freezable' symbol next to them can be safely frozen. If there's no freezer symbol by a recipe, this means that it isn't ideal for freezing.

HOW TO STORE FOOD IN THE FRIDGE
• Store leftovers in airtight containers in the fridge. This slows down the growth of bacteria and helps stop other food flavours leaching into it.

• Fully cool food before putting it in the fridge.

• Cool food as quickly as possible (within 2 hours) by spreading it evenly on a cool surface. If you are storing rice, ensure it is fully cooled and refrigerated within 1 hour of cooking.

• Most cooked food will last for around 2–3 days in the fridge, however, some more perishable foods (such as cooked fish) will last for only 24 hours.

• Always store raw meat on a separate shelf, below fresh fruit, vegetables and any cooked leftovers.

• As a general rule, foods that need to stay dry, like muffins, or foods that do not contain items like meat, fish or rice can be stored at room temperature. If you're in doubt, store in the fridge or a cool place or consult the storage instructions for the specific recipe.

HOW TO STORE FOOD IN THE FREEZER
• Package up all foods in airtight containers or bags to prevent freezer burn. Ideally, remove any excess air from bags and pack boxes tightly, which helps the food keep for longer.

• Freeze in portions, so you can defrost only what you need. To freeze separate small foods, place a small square of non-stick baking paper in between each item to stop them sticking together.

• Label and date the food you put in the freezer.

• Never freeze raw meat or fish twice.

• You can defrost fruit and veg and raw meats, cook with them, then freeze that cooked meal.

• Always store raw frozen meat on a different shelf to frozen fruit and veg, as this may be eaten uncooked.

• Only place cold or cooled food in the freezer.

REHEATING FOOD FROM THE FRIDGE OR FREEZER
Most foods, such as fritters, can be eaten cold after storing in the fridge or defrosting, as long as they were fully cooked previously (with the exception of fruit like berries, which can be eaten uncooked after defrosting). If reheating, follow these instructions:

• When reheating food, ensure it is piping hot before cooling and serving to kill any bacteria.

• Fully defrost frozen food in the fridge before reheating and serving, unless it can be cooked from frozen. Foods which can be cooked from frozen are usually those that aren't easy to overcook, like soup.

• When reheating some foods, you may need to add a splash of extra moisture to avoid it tasting dry; usually water or milk, depending on what was used in the original recipe. This is because a lot of the moisture content in food is lost when reheating.

• If you defrost food at room temperature, keep an eye on it and place in the fridge as soon as it is defrosted, as bacteria can start to grow quicker at room temperature.

• Leftovers should only ever be reheated once.

• Defrosted food should be consumed within 24 hours.

• Do not refreeze food which has already been fully defrosted.

batch cooking

My favourite kind of recipe is one that will feed you now and also again on another day. Batch cooking can help you save time in the kitchen and keep costs down on ingredients while making sure you still have a stock of delicious, nutritious meals on hand when you're at your busiest.

For those of you who love a batch cook, I have dedicated a whole chapter to some ideal batch-cooking recipes from page 62. Plenty of other recipes in this book are also suitable for batch cooking – you can find instructions for how to store and use any leftovers on the left-hand side of each recipe.

Here are my top tips for batch cooking:

Plan ahead – check your freezer stash and make a note of the things you may find useful in the near future – you might want a store of items you can easily grab for packed lunches or picnics, a strong supply of snacks for when the kids are off school or have an impromptu playdate and, best of all for when you have a busy few days, a selection of delicious meals you can quickly pull out of the freezer whenever you need. Make your freezer work to your advantage!

Make sure you have a good stock of storage items to keep your batch cooks as fresh as possible – airtight containers are a must! Non-stick baking paper is always handy to avoid food sticking together so you can just defrost what you need when you need it.

And finally, please don't feel like you need to be batch cooking all the time, these recipes are also great to enjoy on the day you make them. Don't feel the pressure to be always organized – I'm definitely often the opposite!

tips for saving time in the kitchen

Here are a few tips and tricks to help shave moments off the time you spend working away in the kitchen, making cooking for your family a little less stressful.

Plan and shop ahead, so that when you wake up in the morning, you're super clear on what the day's cooking will involve. This might mean mulling over what you'll be having the night before cooking, or making use of a meal plan for each day of the week. Take note of any perishable foods you have that need using up and read any new recipes through in advance so that you know exactly what you're doing and what you'll need. This prep will help you to get on and cook a meal quickly, without any confusion over missing ingredients or pondering your next step.

Pre-boil the kettle My favourite time-saving tip – probably because it's one I use on a daily basis – saves those precious minutes spent waiting for a big pan of water to come to the boil. Simply fill a kettle with the appropriate amount of water for your recipe and put it on to boil. While you are waiting, add about 1cm ($^1/_2$in) of tap water to the saucepan you'll be cooking in, and set this over the highest heat on the hob. Add the boiling water from the kettle, and the pan of water will come back to the boil in a matter of seconds. This is a safe way of ensuring the cold pan won't bring the water temperature down and make the whole process take longer.

Prep your fruits and veggies At the same time as unpacking your shopping, try to get ahead and do some prep. Anything you can fit in will be one less step to do whilst cooking. Wash and dry whole vegetables, wrap them in kitchen paper to soak up any excess moisture and place them in airtight containers. Most non-perishable vegetables like onions, broccoli, carrots and parsnips can be chopped up after washing and placed in an airtight container with damp kitchen paper to prevent drying out. They should last around 2–3 days in the fridge like this. I would avoid pre-prepping veggies or fruit like avocado, which browns easily. If you find that some veggies, like broccoli, carrots and bok choy, are starting to turn later in the week, place in cold water overnight to restore them back to a fresh texture.

Soft fruits, like berries, can be soaked in cold water with a splash of white vinegar for 5 minutes to draw out impurities. Dry them well and transfer to an airtight container lined with kitchen paper to soak up excess moisture. Firmer fruits, like apples and pears, can be washed, dried and kept at room temperature.

Organize your kitchen You might be putting it off, but organizing your kitchen makes for a much less stressful cooking experience. Don't store all your spices at the back of the cupboard, or have the kettle tucked away when you'll need to use it often. I like to keep all my spices in a drawer next to the hob so that they are within easy reach. My most-used pots and pans are also in places that are easy to access.

Pre-prepared or pre-cooked foods such as canned chickpeas and beans, pouches of pre-cooked rice and bags of frozen veg are all invaluable when it comes to saving time in the kitchen. The same goes for quick flavour boosters like garlic paste and garlic granules. Purchasing pre-chopped fresh veg is also an option, though it's often a little more expensive.

Set the little ones up with an activity Do this before you start to cook in the hope that it will minimize distractions from hungry little ones. You will find suggestions of activities dotted throughout this book.

Try to get the best equipment you can afford A good-quality heavy-based, non-stick frying pan is a must because a cheap thin one that everything sticks to and burns won't do you any favours. Likewise, blunt or flimsy peelers or knives will hold you back and require a lot more effort and time.

Find the right mindset My best advice for saving time in the kitchen is to get in the zone. 10 minutes is usually all you need to prep a meal quickly, and if you're someone who doesn't love cooking, find ways to make it more enjoyable. Get some music on or get the kiddos involved and time will fly. Or, simply think about all the delicious food at the end!

keeping kids entertained

We all know how tricky it can be to get the kids to settle sometimes, especially when you need it most! So please don't feel guilty for using the TV or tablet to keep them occupied for a few moments – parent in the way that works for you to keep your sanity! When you have the time and patience, and the kids need a break from the screen, here are a few ideas that you may find helpful to keep them entertained. Of course, please keep in mind the age of your child for each of these, as some items, such as small objects, may not be suitable for smaller children.

Make up a cooking activity bag or basket and attach it to the high chair or stash it near to where you cook. This way, there are always toys on hand to keep the little one occupied while you're distracted for 10 minutes.

Tape small objects like toys, hollow balls, baby cutlery, etc. to baby's high chair tray. It'll keep them occupied for a few moments.

Or simply stick strips of masking or multi-coloured tape to the high chair tray or table and allow your little one to peel it off.

Stuff an array of multicoloured pom-poms into a large whisk and let baby try to pick them out!

Let little ones enjoy food that isn't filling but takes a long time to eat. Like a bowl of pomegranate seeds, rice cakes, small pieces of cereal or cooked cold peas. Baby will spend lots of time practising their pincer grip. This one is especially good when you are eating out and waiting for the food to arrive.

Make a sensory basket filled with kitchen items for baby to play with so they can feel involved with what you're doing. Include items like a metal whisk, a wooden spoon, a smash-proof bowl, etc.

My Nina has always loved a sticker sheet, which keeps her entertained for a little bit. My top tip is to peel away the sticker sheet from the edges, leaving the actual stickers still attached to the backing. This way your little ones can pick off the stickers themselves much easier.

Turn a colander upside down and stick lots of craft feathers into a bunch of the holes, baby can pull them out and enjoy the soft sensory experience.

super fast

Whether you're looking for a speedy yet satisfying breakfast, quick lunch, or comforting evening meal, the recipes in this chapter will show you how to cook dishes the whole family will love, all in 10 minutes or less, so that you can spend less time in the kitchen and more time tackling that never-ending parenting to-do list. Be sure to also check out the No Cook chapter for even more speedy ideas that don't involve any cooking at all.

cinnamon apple toast

I know what you're thinking... it's just toast. No, no, this is next-level toast! It tastes like a delicious cinnamon Danish pastry, but you can make it in 10 minutes. If you have a big family, make a double batch – you won't regret it.

 GF*

 EF

 V

 Vg*

 DF*

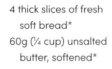

Makes 4 pieces of toast

4 thick slices of fresh soft bread*
60g (¼ cup) unsalted butter, softened*

1 x 90g (3¼oz) pouch of apple purée (see note)

1 tbsp light soft brown sugar (optional)
2 tsp ground cinnamon

Prep 5 minutes, Cook 5–6 minutes

Preheat the grill to high.

Pop the slices of bread in a toaster and toast until they are slightly light brown – you don't want to make it too crisp at this stage so keep an eye on it.

Meanwhile, make the topping. Place the butter in a small bowl, ensuring it is soft enough to mix with the other ingredients. In winter, my kitchen stays too cold for butter to soften at room temperature, so I like to cube it, put it in a bowl, cover and heat on LOW for 30–40 seconds in the microwave until just soft – just be careful not to let it melt completely.

Love your leftovers

These toasts are best served fresh, however leftovers will keep for up to 24 hours. Enjoy cold or reheat in a hot oven for 5 minutes until piping hot throughout.

Add the apple purée, sugar, if using, and cinnamon. Stir well to combine using a tablespoon. Don't worry if the mixture looks slightly separated right now, it will be completely fine.

Once the toast is done, spread a quarter of the butter mixture over each slice, using the back of your tablespoon to ensure you have an even layer and the mixture reaches right to the edges.

Place all the toast on a large baking tray and heat under the preheated grill for around 5 minutes, until the exposed bread edges have browned, and the cinnamon butter is bubbling on top.

It will be hot when it first comes out of the grill, so wait a few moments for the toast to slightly cool, then cut into quarters, or finger strips for little ones to enjoy.

Note If you can't find apple purée pouches, don't worry, any fruit flavour will work. Just ensure it is unsweetened 100% fruit, definitely with no added cereals. Alternatively, a small mashed banana also works.

curried carrot eggy bread

A quick lunch option to add a bit of variety from the everyday sarnie. You could use half a courgette (zucchini) instead of the carrot if that's what you have in the fridge.

Makes 2 large sandwiches

Prep 4 minutes, Cook 5–6 minutes

♡

Love your leftovers

I recommend serving this dish fresh, however, leftovers will keep for up to 24 hours in the fridge. Reheat in the microwave on HIGH for 60 seconds until piping hot, or pop back in the pan to crisp up again.

1 small carrot, washed, peeled if you like
½ tsp mild curry powder
2 heaped tbsp finely grated Emmental cheese (or Cheddar)*
4 thick slices of bread*
2 medium eggs
2 tsp garlic-infused oil

Preheat a large, non-stick frying pan over a medium-high heat.

Meanwhile, finely grate the carrot. Scoop up the carrot pulp in your hand and give it a gentle squeeze to remove most of the excess liquid, then add it to a large bowl. Add the curry powder and grated cheese and give the mixture a good stir to coat the carrot in the spices.

Make 2 sandwiches with the cheesy carrot filling and the thick slices of bread and set these aside.

Whisk the eggs in a wide, flat-bottomed bowl, then place the sandwiches in the beaten egg. Before you get your hands messy, carefully add the oil to the hot frying pan to heat up.

Flip the sandwiches over so the other side of bread soaks up some egg, then transfer the sandwiches to the hot frying pan. To avoid wasting any egg, use your fingers to scrape the last of the egg out of the bowl and onto the top of the sandwiches in the middle, trying not to let any drip down the sides.

Quickly wash your hands, then turn the heat down to medium so the sarnies don't burn. After a minute or so, flip each sandwich over and cook on the other side for 3–4 minutes, until the outsides have browned and the cheese is super melty inside.

Serve cut into quarters or finger strips for little ones with a picky salad and some low-salt and sugar tomato sauce on the side, if you like.

Note For an extra touch of crunch and flavour, add a pinch of grated cheese to the outside of each egg-soaked piece of bread, this will crisp up as the egg cooks.

breakfast burritos two ways

There is something delicious about eggs with various trimmings all wrapped up in a soft tortilla. Even better if you can squeeze a few veggies in there too! Here are two ways to do this. P.S. Adults get the hot sauce ready – it goes perfectly with these. You can see how they look on pages 28–29.

courgette and egg roll-ups

These warm, soft little spirals are perfect for all the family. A quick breakfast, lunch or dinner to satisfy those hungry tummies.

 GF*

 V

 DF*

Serves 1 adult and 1 little

Prep and cook 8 minutes

Freezable

♡

Love your leftovers

This dish is best served fresh, but will keep in the fridge for up to 24 hours, or in the freezer for up to 3 months tightly wrapped in foil. To reheat, place the frozen foil-wrapped roll-up in a hot oven on a baking tray for 10–20 minutes until piping hot throughout.

1 tbsp garlic-infused oil or unsalted butter*
1 small courgette (zucchini)

2 large eggs
40g (1½oz) of your favourite cheese*, grated

1 large soft tortilla wrap*
freshly ground black pepper

Add the oil or butter to a large, lidded, non-stick frying pan over a high heat and let it warm up.

Meanwhile, quickly grate the courgette. Taking handfuls at a time, squeeze the liquid out over the sink, then add the courgette pulp to the hot pan.

Stir, then press down with your spoon or spatula to flatten the grated courgette into an even layer so it cooks quicker. Sauté for 3–5 minutes, stirring and spreading flat every minute or so, until the courgette has softened and all the moisture has evaporated.

Meanwhile, add the eggs, cheese and a little black pepper to a bowl and whisk together well with a fork. Once the courgette is soft, pour the cheesy eggs in and stir immediately to mix the courgette into the eggs. Using a firm rubber spatula, scrape the egg from the base of the pan for 30 seconds while mixing well. Now use your spatula to evenly distribute the courgette across the pan, allowing the uncooked egg to pool across the pan, essentially making a thin omlette. Pop the frying pan lid on, or carefully cover with foil, and steam for 2 minutes to help the top cook through as well as the bottom.

Lay the tortilla flat on a clean work surface, then gently slide the courgette omelette out of the pan and on top of the tortilla. Roll up the tortilla with the omelette inside to make a long sausage, then cut it widthways into 2.5cm (1in) wide pinwheels to serve.

Serve with avocado, plain yogurt and some fruit on the side, if you like.

tomato scrambled egg breakfast burritos

Sweet, juicy tomatoes turn these eggs into flavourful soft pillows – perfect for stuffing inside a burrito!

 GF*

 V

 DF*

Makes 3 large burritos

Prep and cook 10 minutes

Freezable

Love your leftovers

These burritos keep well in the freezer. Wrap each one in a piece of non-stick baking paper, then in a layer of foil and freeze for up to 3 months. To defrost, take off the foil but keep the paper on. Cook on HIGH in the microwave for 2 minutes, then unwrap and fry in a hot frying pan to crisp up the tortilla wrap. Alternatively, place in a hot oven to defrost and reheat for 30–40 minutes.

1 tbsp garlic-infused oil
3 handfuls of sweet cherry tomatoes
1 tsp garlic granules
½ tsp smoked paprika

4 medium eggs, lightly beaten
3 large soft tortilla wraps*
3 tbsp sour cream* (optional)

1–2 ripe avocados, peeled, pitted and sliced
freshly ground black pepper

Add the oil and cherry tomatoes to a large, non-stick frying pan over a high heat. Allow the tomatoes to cook down for 4 minutes, stirring often and pressing down on the tops with a fish slice or spatula to pop the skins and make the flesh turn jammy.

Sprinkle over the garlic granules, paprika and a little black pepper and stir well. Pour the beaten eggs into the pan and use a firm but bendy rubber cake spatula to stir the eggs, scraping them up from the base of the pan and folding over to make light, pillow-like clouds of egg. Try not to over mix as this will result in small chunks of scrambled egg, which is harder for little fingers to enjoy.

The eggs will take no more than 2 minutes to cook, so once they look firm but still have a sheen on the top, take the pan off the heat and set aside.

To assemble the burritos, lay a large tortilla wrap on a clean chopping board or work surface. Add a tablespoon of sour cream to the centre and spread it out slightly in a rectangle shape. Add a third of the tomato scrambled eggs in an even layer to the centre of the tortilla, then top with some avocado slices. Try to keep at least 7.5cm (3in) of tortilla clear around the edge, as you'll need this to roll up the burrito.

Fold in each side, then fold in the bottom edge closest to you. Roll up the burrito, ensuring the sides stay tucked in. Finish with the seam placed down so it doesn't unravel, then cut in half on the diagonal to serve. Repeat to make 3 burritos.

Serve with avocado, plain yogurt and some fruit on the side, if you like. Serve adults a whole burrito and little ones can have a half each to have a go at. You can also serve the elements deconstructed for little ones under 18 months if you prefer, as they may struggle to pick it up.

A note on bread
Offering wholegrain foods like brown bread to baby is safe, however they do tend to fill up little tummies faster, running the risk that baby won't consume all the nutrients they need in their diet. Therefore, serve wholegrain foods to baby in moderation.

courgette toastie

You can never go wrong with a toasted cheese sandwich for lunch. With an irresistible cheesy crust, this one does not disappoint. Plus, it's packed with veggies so it's a win-win!

Makes 2 toasties

Prep 5 minutes, Cook 5 minutes

♡

Love your leftovers

If you have any leftovers, which I highly doubt, store in the fridge for up to 24 hours. Reheat in a frying pan until the cheese inside is piping hot.

1 small courgette (zucchini)
60g (2oz) Cheddar cheese*

50g (¼ cup) cream cheese, mascarpone or super-thick plain yogurt*
1 tsp garlic granules

4 thick slices of bread*
1½ tbsp unsalted butter*, softened
freshly ground black pepper

Place a large, non-stick frying pan over a medium-high heat to warm up.

Quickly grate the courgette, then taking one small handful of grated courgette at a time, squeeze the juice out and add the grated pulp to a bowl. Discard the courgette water from your chopping board, then grate the cheese. Add just over half of the grated cheese to the courgette bowl, reserving some for later.

Add the cream cheese, mascarpone or yogurt, the garlic granules and a good grinding of black pepper to the bowl and mix well. Divide the courgette filling between two slices of bread and spread it out evenly. Top both with another slice of bread each to make two sandwiches.

Spread the top side of both sandwiches with butter, then place the sandwiches, buttered-side down, in the hot frying pan. Spread butter on what is now the top side, then allow the toasties to cook for 2–3 minutes.

Flip the toasties over using a spatula or fish slice, then add a small sprinkling of cheese to the browned top of each. Allow it to melt a little while the toastie cooks for another 2 minutes, then flip again. Add the remaining cheese to the other side of the toastie, and after 30–60 seconds, flip the toastie one last time to crisp it up. The cheese should melt into the bread and turn a delicious golden colour.

Remove the toasties from the pan once they are super golden on the outside and the cheese is all melty inside. Serve immediately for adults, or leave to cool slightly and cut into finger strips for little ones under 3.

These taste great with a little low-salt and sugar tomato sauce for dipping, if you like.

quick tuna sweetcorn pasta

Looking for a simple, quick, fuss-free dinner for the family after a busy day? This tuna pasta is easy to whip up in minutes. Served cold, it's perfect for lunches on the go too.

 GF*

 EF

 DF*

Serves 2 adults and 2 littles

Prep and cook 6 minutes

Love your leftovers

Leftovers will keep for up to 2 days in the fridge. The yogurt may look watery after sitting in the fridge for a little while, but this is totally fine, just give it a good mix again before serving. Yogurt doesn't defrost well, so this dish is best served fresh.

250g (9oz) quick-cook dried pasta* (preferably fusilli)
1 x 260g (9¼oz) can of unsalted sweetcorn in water, drained

2 x 110g (3¾oz) cans of tuna in spring water, drained
juice of ½ a lemon
10 heaped tbsp thick Greek yogurt*

a generous amount of freshly ground black pepper

Cook the pasta in a large saucepan of boiling water according to the packet instructions.

Meanwhile, add the remaining ingredients to a large mixing bowl and give them a good mix until evenly combined.

Once the pasta is done, drain it into a colander over the sink. Place the colander of pasta briefly under the cold running water tap to cool it down. This will stop the pasta from soaking up all of the yogurt. Shake the colander well to drain excess water, then add the cooled pasta to the tuna mixture and mix well to coat it in the sauce.

Serve alongside a picky salad or cooked veg for a simple dinner that's ready in minutes.

Note Feel free to use frozen sweetcorn instead of canned if you like, simply cook the corn according to the packet instructions in the same water as the pasta.

For a sweeter touch
You can also swap 5 tablespoons
of the Greek yogurt for mayo if
you prefer a sweeter taste – just be
mindful that most shop-bought
mayonnaise does contain eggs and
can have a higher salt content,
so serve in moderation
to little ones.

creamy spinach and cheese soup

Rich and comforting, this soup is perfect on a cold winter's day with a big hunk of crusty bread for dipping. Try pairing it with leftover cooked gammon if you have it – it makes the perfect combo!

 GF*
 EF
 V
 Vg*
 DF*

Serves 2 adults and 2 littles

Prep and cook 10 minutes

Freezable

Love your leftovers

Leftovers will keep in the fridge for up to 2 days or freeze in portions for up to 3 months. Defrost on HIGH for 3–4 minutes in the microwave until simmering and piping hot, or defrost thoroughly in the fridge and reheat in a saucepan.

7 cubes of frozen spinach, preferably pre-chopped (see note)
400ml (1⅔ cups) milk*
1 low-salt chicken or vegetable stock cube*
2 tsp garlic granules OR 1 garlic clove, crushed
½–1 tsp Dijon mustard, to taste
1–2 tbsp cornflour (cornstarch), depending on how thick you want the soup
80–100g (2¾–3½oz) smoked Cheddar or Gruyère cheese*, grated
freshly ground black pepper

Fill the kettle and put it on to boil.

Add the spinach cubes to a microwaveable jug with a splash of water. Cover and heat for 2–3 minutes on HIGH until defrosted. Alternatively, you can let the spinach cubes melt in the soup, but the whole dish will take longer to cook.

Meanwhile, set a large saucepan over a high heat and add the milk and 300ml (1¼ cups) of boiling water. Crumble in the stock cube, then add the garlic, Dijon mustard and a generous grinding of black pepper and bring to a simmer.

While you wait, add the cornflour to a small bowl or mug along with a splash of cold water and mix to make a paste.

Pour away most of the excess water from the cooked spinach, then add the spinach to the milk in the pan and bring to a gentle simmer. Once simmering, pour the cornflour slurry all around, stirring immediately to incorporate it. (The milk does need to be piping hot before the cornflour slurry is added or it won't thicken, however, don't allow the milk to boil or it may curdle.) Simmer for a further 2 minutes until the soup has thickened, then remove the pan from the heat.

Add the cheese and stir very well as it melts to avoid curdling, then serve the soup into bowls. For little ones, serve with bread fingers for dipping, or boil some pasta on the side to coat the soup around.

Note If you only have whole leaf frozen spinach (as opposed to chopped), run a knife over the thawed spinach to chop it up, then add to the milk before heating up and adding the cornflour slurry as above. Alternatively, if you only have fresh spinach, finely chop the spinach, then add it to the simmering milk before adding the cornflour.

SUPER FAST

Add extra protein
Once the soup has thickened and before adding the cheese, you can try adding chunks of fish to poach, or cooked shredded chicken to heat through for a little extra protein.

tuna broccoli crumpet hash

 GF*

 DF*

This is one of those dishes that may not always look the prettiest, but it's very yummy, easy and includes veg. Everyone will enjoy it, so what's not to love?!

Serves 1 adult and 1 little

Prep 4 minutes, Cook 6 minutes

Freezable

Love your leftovers

Leftovers will keep for up to 1 day in the fridge or 3 months in the freezer. Defrost thoroughly in the fridge, then put back in a frying pan with a little more oil to crisp up and reheat until piping hot throughout.

3 medium eggs
1 x 110g (3¾oz) can of tuna in spring water, drained
2 crumpets* (or 2 thick slices of bread*)
4 fresh medium–large broccoli florets
40g (1½oz) Cheddar cheese*, finely grated
1 tbsp garlic-infused oil
freshly ground black pepper

Place a large, non-stick frying pan over a high heat to warm up.

Meanwhile, add the eggs and the tuna to a large bowl and whisk them together, breaking up any larger lumps of tuna. Quickly cut the crumpets (or bread) up into 1cm (½in) cubes – no need to be precise. Add the crumpets to the egg in the bowl.

Now take each broccoli floret and use a large, sharp knife to finely chop the flowery head on each one, saving the stalks for another recipe. You want the bits of broccoli to be very finely shredded, otherwise they won't soften well. Add the broccoli to the crumpets and egg along with the cheese and a little black pepper, then give it all a good stir.

Add the oil to the now-hot pan, then pour the egg mixture into the pan, using a spatula to scrape out any remaining bits from the bowl. Spread the mixture flat so the pieces of crumpet lay evenly, then let it cook for 2–3 minutes. Refrain from prodding and poking it as this will slow down the cooking process.

Now if you're brave, shake the pan to ensure it's not stuck and flip the lot like a pancake. Alternatively, use a fish slice or spatula to flip it in sections. Leave the other side to cook for a further 2–3 minutes, pressing down on the top of the eggy crumpets with the back of a spatula so that there's lots of contact with the hot pan.

When there is 1 minute left of the cooking time, roughly break the mixture up into smaller pieces and give it a little stir before serving with a picky salad. Adults, this one is delicious with a good dollop of hot sauce for dunking, and for the kiddos serve with plain yogurt.

Veggie swaps Replace the broccoli with finely grated carrot or parsnip for a little variety. You can also use coarsely grated courgette, just squeeze the excess liquid out before adding to the eggs.

cheesy garlic butter chicken tacos

Cheesy garlic bread is one of my all-time favourite flavour combos, and these tacos don't disappoint! The juicy and succulent chicken pieces have a flavourful, garlicky coating which is moreishly soft in some parts and crunchy in others. A must for a quick, midweek meal that will have everyone going back for seconds.

Makes approx. 8 tacos

Prep and cook 10 minutes

Freezable

Love your leftovers

Leftover chicken will keep in the fridge for up to 2 days, or in the freezer for up to 2 months. Defrost in the fridge, then reheat in the oven or frying pan until piping hot throughout.

1 tbsp cornflour (cornstarch)
600g (1lb 5oz) skinless boneless chicken breasts or thighs, diced into 2–3cm (¾–1¼in) chunks
1 tbsp unsalted butter*
1 tsp garlic-infused oil

1 tsp dried mixed herbs
2 tsp garlic granules
50g (1¾oz) Cheddar cheese*
2 garlic cloves, crushed OR 1 heaped tsp garlic purée
freshly ground black pepper

To serve
8 soft mini tortilla wraps*
Greek yogurt or a dip* (see pages 213–214)
shredded lettuce
gherkins (pickles) and/ or my Japanese Smacked Cucumber Pickle (see page 215)

Set a large, non-stick frying pan over a high heat to warm up.

Meanwhile, add the cornflour to the chicken in the open container it came in (to save time and washing up) and toss until the chicken is evenly coated.

Once the frying pan is hot, add the butter and oil, then the chicken. Spread the chicken into one even layer and cover it with a good grinding of black pepper. Leave to cook for 4 minutes without touching the chicken so it can get some good colour on the outside.

Now is a good time to whip up an accompaniment to go with your tacos. I recommend my Japanese Smacked Cucumber Pickle (see page 215).

Once the 4 minutes is up, give the frying pan a toss to flip most of the chicken pieces over, then cook for 1 further minute.

Add the dried herbs and garlic granules to the chicken and stir well. Grab the cheese and grate it directly into the pan, coating all the chicken in a layer of cheese which should melt almost instantly. Toss the pan again and cook for a further 4 minutes, stirring every 1 minute. Allow the chicken plenty of contact with the hot pan between stirs, as this gives it delicious crispy bits.

At the last minute, add the fresh garlic or garlic purée and give the pan another toss. Cook for 1 final minute before serving.

When serving these tacos, I like to add bowls of various fillings to my dining table so everyone can assemble their own food. It's especially exciting for kids and helps them to feel more in control of their food. To assemble your tacos, add a small pile of chicken to the middle of a tortilla wrap and top with your choice of fillings. For little ones, serve everything deconstructed, with the chicken pieces cut in half and the wrap cut into strips.

saucy lemon butter chicken

Citrusy, silky and flavourful. It takes just 10 minutes to whip up this flavour-packed meal!

 GF*

 EF

 DF*

Serves 2 adults and 2 littles

Prep and cook 10 minutes

Freezable

Love your leftovers

Leftovers will keep for up to 2 days in the fridge, or you can freeze the mixture (before adding to pasta) for up to 3 months – pasta is best cooked fresh. Defrost thoroughly before adding a splash more water and simmering in a saucepan until the chicken is piping hot throughout.

200g (7oz) dried pasta of your choice*
1 tbsp garlic-infused oil
approx. 500g (1lb 2oz) skinless boneless chicken breasts, cut into mini fillet strips

1 unwaxed lemon
2 large garlic cloves
1 low-salt chicken stock cube*
2 tbsp maple syrup (optional)
1 heaped tbsp cornflour (cornstarch)

30g (2 tbsp) unsalted butter, cubed*
50g (1¼oz) Cheddar*, grated (optional)
freshly ground black pepper

Put a full kettle on boil and preheat a large, non-stick frying pan over the highest heat. In a large saucepan, start cooking the pasta according to the packet instructions, reserving 175ml (¾ cup) of boiled water in the kettle.

Add the garlic oil, then the chicken strips to the now-hot frying pan in an even layer. Allow the chicken to cook for 8 minutes, flipping the pieces over halfway through. Don't touch the chicken pieces as they cook, as this slows down the process and you'll lose that delicious, caramelized golden crust if you move them about too much.

While the chicken cooks, prep the sauce. Finely grate the lemon zest. Skip a step and don't bother peeling the garlic cloves, just cut away the hard stems and finely grate them, the papery skin will fall away as you do so.

Add the grated lemon zest and garlic to a measuring jug and crumble in the stock cube. Pour in 175ml (¾ cup) of boiling water from the kettle and stir well to dissolve the stock cube. Halve the lemon and squeeze all the juice into the jug of chicken stock, catching any pips that escape. Add the maple syrup, if using, and a good grinding of black pepper.

By this time the chicken should be pretty much cooked. Sprinkle the cornflour over the chicken and give it a quick toss. Add the butter to the pan and allow it to melt, then toss the chicken to coat it all over in the melted butter. You shouldn't be able to see any dry bits of cornflour.

Now quickly pour in your lemony chicken stock and stir and toss the contents of the pan continuously for 1 minute until the sauce is well thickened. Finally, add the grated cheese, if desired, and let it melt into the sauce. Add the drained, cooked pasta to the chicken and sauce and stir to coat well.

Top with an extra grinding of black pepper and a sprinkling of salt for the adults. For little ones under the age of 3, cut the chicken into finger strips before serving.

Note If you fancy a change from pasta, this saucy chicken is just as delicious served with veggies and boiled potatoes or rice.

speedy prawn pasta

If you're in a hurry and fancy a tomato-based, creamy pasta sauce for dinner, which is a fab carrier for your proteins or veggies, then look no further. Put approximately 6 minutes of work in and dinner is served! This recipe includes prawns, but feel free to leave them out for a simple veggie pasta dish.

GF*

EF

V*

DF*

Serves 1 adult and 2 littles

Prep and cook 6 minutes

Freezable

Love your leftovers

Leftovers with prawns will keep for up to 24 hours in the fridge, or up to 3 days without the prawns. As this sauce is so quick to make, I recommend not freezing it as the pasta will soften. However, if you wish to freeze leftovers, use raw prawns instead of ready-cooked (see note) and keep leftovers in the freezer for up to 3 months. Defrost in the microwave with a splash of water and reheat until piping hot.

150g (5½oz) quick-cook dried pasta* (any shape you like)

2 big handfuls of frozen vegetables of your choice

1 tsp garlic-infused oil

3 tbsp tomato purée (paste)

1 garlic clove, crushed OR 1 tsp garlic granules

1 tsp smoked paprika

pinch of sugar (optional)

150g (⅔ cup) cream cheese*

150ml (⅔ cup) milk*

170g (6oz) ready-cooked fresh peeled prawns (shrimp)*

50g (1¾oz) Cheddar cheese*, grated (optional)

freshly ground black pepper

Bring a large saucepan of water to the boil using boiling water from the kettle to speed up the process. Check the instructions on the packets of pasta and frozen veg and cook them together in the boiling water so that they are ready at the same time.

Meanwhile, set a large frying pan over a medium-high heat and add the garlic oil. Squeeze in the tomato purée, then add the fresh garlic or garlic granules, smoked paprika, sugar, if using, and a little black pepper. Stir well with a wooden spoon and cook for 2 minutes to reduce the acidity in the tomato purée, which will give the dish a sweeter finish.

Now spoon in the cream cheese and stir well until melted. Add the milk to thin the consistency of the sauce. Add the prawns and cook for 1–2 minutes to heat them through. If the sauce is still too thick, add a splash of the pasta cooking water and stir well. To check the prawns are piping hot inside, cut one open and place your finger on the flesh inside, if it feels piping hot, they're done. Remove the pan from the heat, stir in the grated cheese and let it melt.

Drain the pasta and veg, then add them to the pan and toss well to coat them in the sauce.

Serve immediately, with extra salt and pepper on the adult portions. For little ones under 18 months, the prawns can be served whole or chopped into pieces no bigger than 1cm (½in). Chop up any bigger pieces of veg into smaller pieces or mash them with the back of a fork before serving to baby.

Note If you plan on freezing leftovers, use raw unfrozen peeled prawns (instead of ready-cooked) and cook them in the sauce for 3–5 minutes until pink throughout before adding the pasta.

crispy pork pittas

A real family sharing meal that's ready in a jiffy. This recipe uses pork mince, but feel free to use any other meat in mince form, or even swap for leftover meat or roasted veggies from your Sunday roast. Growing up, I used to love the Monday leftovers after the Sunday roast. Shred the meat and add it to the frying pan with the spices and cook until it's crispy.

 GF*

 EF

 V*

 DF*

Makes 6 pittas

Prep and cook 10 minutes

Freezable

Love your leftovers

Leftover pork will keep for up to 2 days in the fridge or for up to 3 months in the freezer. Defrost thoroughly in the fridge, then reheat in a hot frying pan until it's piping hot throughout.

2 tbsp garlic-infused oil
500g (1lb 2oz) lean minced (ground) pork*
1 tsp ground cumin
2 tsp smoked paprika
2 tsp garlic granules
1 tsp dried mixed herbs
1 heaped tbsp sesame seeds

1 low-salt chicken stock cube*
1 small orange or satsuma
1 tbsp honey for over 1s or maple syrup (optional)
6 soft pitta breads*
freshly ground black pepper

To serve
shredded lettuce
thinly sliced cucumber and carrot
gherkins/pickles (optional)
Japanese Smacked Cucumber Pickle (see page 215)
Greek yogurt or a dip* (see pages 213–214)

Set a large frying pan over a high heat until it is smoking hot.

Add the garlic oil, then the pork. Use a wooden spoon to flatten the mince so it spreads out and fills the frying pan. While the meat begins to crisp up underneath, sprinkle over the cumin, paprika, garlic granules, dried herbs and sesame seeds. Add a generous grinding of black pepper, crumble over the stock cube, then stir everything together well. Use the tip of the wooden spoon to break up the meat until you can't see any large pieces. Allow the meat to cook for 6 minutes, stirring every 2–3 minutes. After each stir, press down on the meat with your spoon to flatten it into an even layer. Try not to stir too much, you want the meat to sit still between stirs so that it can caramelize, rather than stew and become chewy.

Once the meat all looks crispy, cut the orange or satsuma in half and squeeze all the juice into the pan, catching any pips. Add the honey or maple syrup, if using. Give it all a final toss and allow to caramelize for another couple of minutes.

Meanwhile, pop the pitta breads in a warm oven for 5 minutes to heat up, or toast them slightly in batches. Add the shredded lettuce, thinly sliced cucumber and any gherkins and/or pickles of your choice to serving bowls. I like to place all the pitta accompaniments in the middle of the dinner table so that everyone can help themselves and build their own.

To assemble, slice open a warm pitta bread and add a dollop of yogurt or dip. Spoon in a generous amount of the pork, followed by a little lettuce, cucumber and pickles. Add more yogurt or dip on top if you like and enjoy!

For little taste testers, serve deconstructed with some yogurt to dip.

speedy broccoli noodles

Noodles are always a hit with my Nina, they're also super quick to whip up and a great carrier for any veggies you have in. If you fancy bulking out this meal a little further with some protein, fry some prawns, tofu or chicken, then remove them from the pan and add back in with the noodles to reheat once the sauce has thickened.

 GF*
 EF*
 V
 Vg*
 DF

Serves 2 adults and 2 littles

Prep and cook 8 minutes

Freezable

Love your leftovers

This dish is really best served fresh, however, leftovers will keep for up to 2 days in the fridge and can be reheated in a pan with more water and soy sauce. It will also keep in the freezer for up to 3 months. Add a generous splash of water or stock to the fully defrosted noodles and heat, covered, in the microwave on HIGH for 2–3 minutes until piping hot.

1 large head of broccoli, cut into small florets
170g (6oz) medium egg noodles* (or rice noodles)
1 low-salt vegetable stock cube*
2 tbsp low-salt soy sauce*
1 tsp sesame oil
1 tbsp sesame seeds
2 garlic cloves, crushed
1 tbsp dried porcini mushroom powder (optional)
1 heaped tbsp cornflour (cornstarch)
1 tbsp apple cider vinegar

Bring a large saucepan of water to the boil using water from the kettle to speed things up. Add the broccoli florets and cook for 5 minutes.

Add the noodles to the boiling water and cook according to the packet instructions, trying to time it so that the noodles and broccoli will be done at the same time.

Meanwhile, set a large frying pan or wok over a high heat to warm up.

Add 300ml (1¼ cups) of cold water to a medium-sized bowl. Crumble in the stock cube, add the soy sauce, sesame oil, sesame seeds, garlic, mushroom powder if you have it, cornflour and vinegar. Give the mixture a very good stir and pour it into the now-hot pan. Stir well to allow any lumps to melt into the sauce, it should start to thicken imminently.

Quickly drain the noodles and broccoli, which should be done by now. Add them to the frying pan or work with the sauce. Immediately toss and stir to coat the noodles and broccoli in the sauce and then serve.

Adults, if you like a little bit more of a kick, add more soy sauce and some chilli oil or chilli sauce to your portion.

quick prawn coconut curry

Full of Thai inspired flavours, this prawn curry is super quick to whip up. You can add a smashed lemongrass stick into the curry to ramp up the flavour if you wish.

Serves 2 adults and 1 little

Prep and cook 10 minutes

Freezable

Love your leftovers

Leftovers will keep in the fridge for up to 24 hours, or freeze for up to 3 months. Defrost thoroughly before reheating in a saucepan until the prawns and sauce are piping hot.

1 tbsp garlic-infused oil
1 tsp sesame oil
1 heaped tbsp cornflour (cornstarch)
1 tsp garlic paste
1 tsp ginger paste

2 tsp mild curry powder
1 x 400g (14oz) can of coconut milk
2 handfuls of sugar snap peas

1 tsp light soft brown sugar (optional)
300g (10½oz) fresh raw prawns (shrimp), peeled and deveined
1 lime, to serve

Add the garlic oil and sesame oil to a large, high-sided frying pan and heat over a medium-high heat until hot.

Add the cornflour, garlic paste, ginger paste and curry powder. Stir well and allow it to simmer for 30–60 seconds, taking care not to let the spices burn.

Add the coconut milk, stir and bring to the boil. The sauce should thicken fairly instantly as it heats up.

Once the sauce is bubbling, add the sugar snap peas and the brown sugar, if using. Stir well, then add the prawns. Simmer for 5–7 minutes until the prawns are pink, firm and cooked throughout.

Serve over boiled jasmine rice with a wedge of lime on the side, or with flatbreads for dunking – delicious!

If little ones are enjoying this meal with you, you can halve the sugar snap peas lengthways to expose the peas inside. Serve the prawns whole if you have used nice large ones. Otherwise, chop smaller prawns into 1cm (½in) bite-sized pieces or blend them into the coconut sauce in a food processor. Adults, feel free to add a dash of chilli sauce, or even a good dollop of crispy chilli oil goes perfectly in this curry!

creamed corn pasta

Naturally sweet corn pairs so well with creamy cheese and pasta in this quick teatime treat.

Serves 2 adults and 2 littles

Prep and cook 10 minutes

Freezable

Love your leftovers

Leftovers will keep for up to 2 days in the fridge or freeze for up to 3 months. Defrost thoroughly and then reheat in a saucepan with an extra splash of milk until piping hot throughout.

200g (7oz) dried rigatoni pasta*
1¾ tbsp unsalted butter*
approx. 500g (3¼ cups) unsalted drained sweetcorn, canned or defrosted

1 tbsp cornflour (cornstarch)
2 garlic cloves, crushed
1 tsp smoked paprika
150g (⅔ cup) mascarpone cheese*
120ml (½ cup) milk*

80g (2¾oz) Cheddar cheese*, grated
freshly ground black pepper

Boil the kettle and pour the water into a large pot. Bring the water back to the boil, add the pasta and cook according to the packet instructions.

Meanwhile, melt the butter in a large saucepan and add the sweetcorn. Cook for 4–5 minutes until the corn is piping hot, stirring often so the heat is evenly distributed between the kernels. Now add the cornflour, crushed garlic, smoked paprika and a good grinding of black pepper. Stir well until the cornflour has dissolved.

Add the mascarpone and milk and stir until a thick sauce has developed. Take the pan off the heat, then add the grated cheese and stir until it's completely melted.

Scoop the cooked pasta out of the water and transfer it to the sauce using a large pasta spoon which holds a good amount of the starchy water too, as we want this starchy water to loosen the sauce. If you don't have a suitable spoon, drain the pasta, reserving a touch of the cooking water, then add the cooked pasta to the sauce along with a splash of the cooking water. Toss together and serve.

Whole sweetcorn kernels can be served from the age of 6 months, however, if you wish you can use a stick blender to blend the sauce up slightly before adding it to the pasta, this is delicious too.

Note Make it super, SUPER quick by using quick-cook pasta to whip this dish up in under 6 minutes.

10-minute dahl

You can make this dahl really quickly by cooking the lentils and spices separately, then combining them at the last minute. It's a fantastic side dish but also flavourful enough to be the main element of your family meal.

Serves 2 adults and 2 littles as a main

Prep and cook 10 minutes

Freezable

Love your leftovers

Leftovers will keep for up to 2–3 days in an airtight container in the fridge. Reheat in a saucepan or covered in the microwave, stirring often, until piping hot throughout. You can also freeze the dahl for up to 4 months. Defrost and reheat in the microwave in a covered bowl for around 4 minutes, stopping to stir often, until there are no cold spots and the dahl is bubbling.

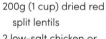

200g (1 cup) dried red split lentils
2 low-salt chicken or vegetable stock cubes*
2 tbsp garlic-infused oil
2 tsp ground turmeric
3 tsp mild curry powder

2 tsp garam masala (a mild blend)
2 garlic cloves, finely grated
a thumb-sized piece of fresh ginger, peeled and grated (optional)

1 x 500g (1lb 2oz) passata (strained tomatoes)
2 tsp golden granulated sugar (optional)
coriander (cilantro), to garnish

Fill the kettle and put it on to boil. Set a large saucepan over a high heat with a touch of tap water at the bottom – it should begin boiling quickly. Meanwhile, open the passata so it is ready to pour when you need it later.

Add the lentils to a fine-mesh sieve and hold under very, very hot running tap water for 1 minute, stirring with a wooden spoon (if you don't have asbestos fingers). You want to wash away the starch until the water runs clear, plus the application of hot water now will make the entire cooking process quicker.

Once washed, add the lentils to the now very hot saucepan. Top up the pan with boiling water from the kettle to cover the lentils by about 2.5cm (1in). Crumble in one of the stock cubes, stir and allow to bubble for 6–7 minutes until the lentils are soft.

When the lentils are nearly ready, set a large, non-stick frying pan over a high heat. Add the garlic oil, followed by the spices, garlic and ginger. Cook for 30 seconds, stirring with a wooden spoon to ensure they don't burn, then as the aromas are released, quickly pour in the passata. It will bubble, so give it a swift stir to incorporate the spiced oil into the tomatoes. Crumble the remaining stock cube into the tomatoes and add the sugar, if using, to help cut through the acidity of the tomatoes, and stir to dissolve.

The lentils should be cooked by now. Use a spoon to scoop a few out to taste – they should be soft with no crunchy graininess. Drain the lentils in a sieve, then immediately add them to the frying pan with the passata mix. Stir together and cook for 1 final minute. Garnish with a sprinkle of freshly chopped coriander and serve with rice or flatbreads, if you like.

This dahl also goes really well with the Spiced Salmon and Veggie Tray Bake (see page 124).

SUPER FAST

fish pie gnocchi

Creamy, smoky, rich and comforting. This meal is prepped and cooked in under 10 minutes and will leave the whole family feeling full and happy. It has fish pie vibes, because it uses similar ingredients to the classic, but with gnocchi instead of potato. This version is much quicker and easier to make than a traditional fish pie – a real winner.

 GF*

 EF

DF*

Serves 2 adults and 2 littles

Prep and cook 8 minutes

Freezable

Love your leftovers

Leftovers will keep for up to 24 hours in the fridge or up to 3 months in the freezer. Defrost thoroughly, then cover and microwave or bake in the oven until piping hot throughout. You can add a splash of milk if it feels very thick. Be mindful that the fish is likely to overcook on reheating, but it will still be safe to eat.

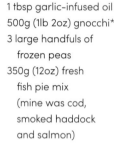

1 tbsp garlic-infused oil
500g (1lb 2oz) gnocchi*
3 large handfuls of frozen peas
350g (12oz) fresh fish pie mix (mine was cod, smoked haddock and salmon)

165g (5¾oz) fresh peeled prawns (shrimp)
300ml (1¼ cups) crème fraîche* or dairy-free plain yogurt
200ml (scant 1 cup) milk*
2 tbsp cornflour (cornstarch)

2 tsp garlic granules
2 tsp unsalted butter*
approx. 60g (2oz) smoked Cheddar cheese*
freshly ground black pepper

Boil the kettle and pour the water into a large saucepan to bring back to the boil.

While you are waiting for the water to boil, set a very large frying pan over a high heat and add the garlic oil to warm up.

Add the gnocchi and frozen peas to the boiling water, then stir and allow to cook for approx. 5 minutes, or until the gnocchi is floating.

While the gnocchi is cooking, add the fish pie mix in an even layer to the hot frying pan. Allow it to cook for 3 minutes, then using a thin sturdy spatula, turn the pieces of fish over to cook on the other side. Don't worry if the fish flakes a touch as you turn it, but it's tastiest if you can keep it as whole as possible. Add the prawns and cook for a further 2 minutes.

Meanwhile, quickly make the sauce. Add the crème fraîche, milk, cornflour and garlic granules to a jug. Whisk the ingredients together using a fork or a mini whisk, ensuring all the cornflour has dissolved.

Once the prawns are looking half-cooked (a little pink in parts but still grey in others), add the butter to the pan and allow it to melt for 30 seconds, before pouring in the crème fraîche sauce.

Use the spatula to gently stir the fish into the sauce. Grate the cheese into the pan, then add some black pepper and stir again. The sauce will be thickening quickly. By now the gnocchi and peas should be cooked, so drain them and add them to the sauce. Stir everything together gently and serve.

This dish is suitable to serve as finger food from 6 months, however, if you wish you can also blend it into a lumpy purée to serve to baby with a spoon.

Pasta swaps
You can swap the gnocchi for pasta, if you prefer. Just cook it following the packet instructions and add the peas with 5 minutes remaining.

kung pao chicken

This one is a really delicious fake-away. What's even more satisfying is that it's ready in just 10 minutes flat.

Serves 2 adults and 2 little ones

Prep and cook 10 minutes

Freezable

Love your leftovers

Leftovers will keep for up to 2 days in the fridge or in the freezer for up to 3 months. Defrost and then reheat in the microwave for 3–4 minutes, stirring once or twice until piping hot.

3 tbsp garlic-infused oil
1 level + 1 heaped tbsp cornflour (cornstarch)
500g (1lb 2oz) skinless boneless chicken breasts or thighs*, cut into 2.5cm (1in) chunks (see note)

1 large red pepper, deseeded and sliced
cooked rice and vegetables, to serve

For the sauce
1 low-salt chicken stock cube*
1 tsp sesame oil

1 tsp ginger paste
1 tsp garlic paste
2 tbsp low-salt soy sauce*
1 tbsp balsamic vinegar
1 tbsp honey or sugar for under 1's (optional)

Add 2 tablespoons of the garlic-infused oil to a large, non-stick frying pan and set it over the highest heat setting on the hob to warm up.

Sprinkle a level tablespoon of cornflour over the chicken in a bowl and toss until it's evenly coated. Add the chicken to the pan in an even layer, ensuring every piece is touching the base of the pan. Fry the chicken for 5–6 minutes, tossing once halfway through. It's important to leave the chicken to cook without touching it too much, if you move it too much it'll release the juices and boil rather than fry.

Meanwhile, make the sauce. Crumble the stock cube into a jug, then add the sesame oil, ginger and garlic pastes, soy sauce, balsamic vinegar and honey or sugar, if using. Stir well, then add 300ml (1¼ cups) of boiling water, stirring again to dissolve the stock cube.

Now the chicken should be cooked and golden, so push the meat to one side of the pan and add the remaining tablespoon of oil to the empty side. Add the pepper slices and cook for 2 minutes until they are softened a little. Sprinkle the remaining heaped tablespoon of cornflour in over the peppers and chicken and stir it all together to allow the cornflour to melt. Cook for 30 seconds, stirring well. Pour in the sauce and allow it to bubble up and thicken, which should take a few minutes.

It's now ready to serve over a bed of rice, and with some veggies or salad on the side. Adults, you may like an extra splash of soy sauce on your portion or a little sprinkling of salt.

Veggie swaps Replace the chicken with firm cubed tofu and sprinkle with an extra level tablespoon of cornflour before frying to help it crisp up.

lemony leek linguine

Naturally sweet leeks are the perfect partner to balance out the tartness of the lemon in this dish. And, really, you can use any pasta shape you like for this simple midweek dinner – I just liked the alliteration so I'm sticking with linguine!

 GF*
 EF
 V*
 Vg*
 DF*

Serves 2 adults and 2 littles

Prep and cook 10 minutes

Freezable

Love your leftovers

Leftovers will keep for up to 2 days in the fridge, or freeze for up to 3 months. Defrost thoroughly and reheat in a saucepan, or blast in the microwave from frozen for 3–4 minutes on HIGH, stirring often until piping hot throughout. You may need to add a splash of water or milk to loosen the consistency when reheating.

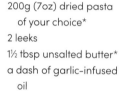

200g (7oz) dried pasta of your choice*
2 leeks
1½ tbsp unsalted butter*
a dash of garlic-infused oil

1 low-salt chicken or vegetable stock cube*
grated zest and juice of ½ unwaxed lemon
2 garlic cloves, crushed
1 tbsp cornflour (cornstarch)

200ml (scant 1 cup) milk*
50g (1¾oz) hard melting cheese, like smoked Cheddar or Parmesan* (optional)
freshly ground black pepper, to taste

Cook the pasta in a large saucepan of boiling water according to the packet instructions. While the pasta is cooking, set a separate large frying pan over a medium-high heat.

Run a sharp knife down the length of each leek, keeping the roots still attached, then wash the leeks under a cold running tap, with the root facing upwards so any soil washes out.

Slice the leeks using a large, sharp knife, as thinly as you can (discard the roots). Add the butter to the hot frying pan along with the oil, which stops the butter from burning. Add the sliced leeks, a little grinding of black pepper and crumble in the stock cube. Sauté for 2–3 minutes, stirring often until the leeks have softened.

Add the lemon zest, garlic and cornflour to the leeks. Stir very well to dissolve the cornflour, then add the lemon juice to the pan. Cook for 1–2 minutes, ensuring all the lemon juice cooks off, which will stop the milk from curdling in the next step.

The leeks should look deliciously caramelized and soft now. Stir the leeks well with a wooden spoon in one hand, then use your other hand to gradually add the milk, stirring continuously to avoid the sauce turning lumpy or splitting.

Once all the milk is incorporated and the sauce is creamy, remove the pan from the heat and add your favourite melty cheese – I love smoked Cheddar in this dish. Stir well to melt the cheese.

Now the pasta should be cooked, so use a large pasta spoon or slotted spoon to scoop the pasta into the leek sauce along with a touch of the cooking water, and toss to coat well.

Season with freshly ground black pepper, to taste. Serve as is, or with a sprinkling of salt for the grown-ups.

peanut butter and banana oaty mug cake

When you fancy a sweet treat and need to satisfy the craving right away, try this gooey peanut butter and banana cake – it's ready in just 7–8 minutes!

 GF*
 EF*
 V
 Vg*
 DF*

Makes 1 large or 2 small mug cakes

1 small very ripe banana
1 tsp light soft brown sugar (optional)
2 tbsp self-raising flour*
2 tbsp rolled porridge oats*

¼ tsp baking powder*
½ tsp vanilla extract
1 tbsp smooth peanut butter (100% nuts) or other nut or seed butter (optional)

1½ tbsp sunflower oil (or any other flavourless oil or melted butter*)
1 medium egg*
sprinkle of chocolate chips* (optional)

Prep 5 minutes, Cook 2 minutes

Mash the banana well with a fork in a large microwaveable mug (or in a small bowl if making 2 cakes). Add the remaining ingredients, apart from the chocolate chips, and mix well. If you are making 2 cakes, decant the mixture into 2 small microwaveable mugs. Sprinkle the choc chips over the top, if using.

Love your leftovers

These are best served fresh as leftovers don't keep well – good job they're so easy to make!

If you are making one large cake, microwave on HIGH for 2–2½ minutes. Carefully remove the mug from the microwave after 2 minutes and check the cake – if the top feels very squidgy, then place it back in the microwave for a further 20–30 seconds. If you are making 2 smaller cakes, microwave these, one at a time, for 60–90 seconds, or until firm on top.

Note that the cakes will rise above the top of the mug and then sink back down again as they cool. Don't worry, they shouldn't spill over.

Serve with a spoon and enjoy!

Note This recipe has been developed using a 950W microwave – please adjust the timings slightly if the power of your microwave is any different.

Fruity swaps
Allergic to narnas? Swap for
a 90g (3¼oz) pouch of fruit
purée found in the baby aisle.
Any fruit will work, but I like to
choose naturally sweeter
flavours like mango. Go for
unsweetened pouches with
no added salt or cereals.

batch cooking

From lunchbox saviours you can easily grab for meals on the go, to snacks for when the kids are off school and meals you can quickly pull out of the freezer whenever you need. The recipes in this chapter are perfect for serving a crowd or for keeping in the freezer stash to save time another day – future you will thank you! See page 17 for my top tips on batch cooking.

store cupboard peach pancakes

GF*
EF*
V
Vg*
DF*

Pancakes are perfect for batch cooking. Make a huge pile of them for brekkie, then the leftovers can be stored in the freezer for fuss-free mornings in the future. You could even add a frozen pancake to the kiddos' lunch box wrapped in non-stick baking paper, it'll be defrosted by lunchtime and delicious!

Makes approx. 20 pancakes

1 x 410g (14oz) can of
  peaches in fruit juice
120g (scant 1 cup)
  self-raising flour*
1½ tsp baking powder*

40g (generous ⅓ cup)
  rolled porridge oats*
2 tsp vanilla extract
3 medium eggs*

2 tbsp melted unsalted
  butter* OR
  flavourless oil like
  sunflower
2 tbsp milk*

Prep 10 minutes, Bake 10–13 minutes

Preheat the oven to 180°C fan (200°C/400°F/Gas 6).

Open the can of peaches slightly, then pour most of the juice away to discard or drink separately, leaving a little bit of juice in the can. Add the peaches and small amount of juice to a large mixing bowl. Using a potato masher, briefly crush the peaches to break them down into small lumps. You don't need to worry too much about the size – a chunky peach purée with a good few large lumps is perfect. Add all the remaining ingredients to the bowl and stir until they are just combined and form a batter.

Freezable

Now, you have a few options for how to cook these pancakes. My favourite is to pour the batter into a large baking tray lined with non-stick baking paper. Spread the batter out in an even layer. Try to make it approx 1.5cm (⅝in) in thickness, but if it's a little thicker or thinner then that's completely fine. Bake in the preheated oven for 10–13 minutes until golden on top. Remove from the oven and allow the pancake to cool for a minute in the tray before cutting into 20 squares using a pizza cutter.

Love your leftovers

The pancakes will keep for up to 3 days in an airtight container at room temperature. Reheat in the toaster or in the oven until piping hot or enjoy them cold. You can also wrap the pancakes in non-stick baking paper and freeze for up to 3 months. Allow to defrost at room temperature and enjoy cold, or reheat in the toaster or microwave until piping hot throughout.

Alternatively, you can bake this mixture in muffin form. Spoon the mixture into either a 24-hole mini muffin tray or a regular 12-hole muffin tray – ideally silicone or a well-greased metal tray. Bake for 10 minutes (mini muffins) or 20 minutes (regular muffins), until they have puffed up and turned golden.

Or, if you want to be traditional, you can opt for standard flat pancake rounds. Fry spoonfuls of the batter in batches in a large, non-stick frying pan over a medium high heat with a little oil. Cook for 2–3 minutes on one side until you can see bubbles forming on the top, then flip and cook for a further minute.

For little ones, serve the pancakes in finger strips with a little yogurt for dipping and fruit. The big kids can have a little honey drizzled on theirs.

Ramp up the extras
To increase the nutritional value, add a tablespoon of chia seeds, ground flax seeds, ground almonds or nut butter. As a general rule, add the same amount of extra milk for each dry ingredient.

Pastry swaps
You can also use puff pastry to make these pop tarts, which gives a softer, flakier texture.

strawberry pop tarts

This American classic is known as a sugary-sweet breakfast treat. It's tasty, but not ideal for our little ones. Why not make this low-sugar version that is even more delicious?

 GF*
 EF*
 V
 Vg*
 DF*

Makes 6 large pop tarts

Prep 10 minutes, Bake 15–20 minutes

Freezable

Love your leftovers

Undecorated pop tarts and pop tarts with the traditional icing will keep for 3–4 days in a sealed container. If you've chosen the yogurt and fruit topping, decorate each pop tart just before serving. Undecorated pop tarts can be frozen for up to 3 months. Defrost thoroughly, then bake at 180°C fan (200°C/400°F/ Gas 6) for 5–10 minutes until piping hot to minimize any soggy pastry.

220g (8oz) strawberries, roughly chopped
1 tbsp maple syrup (optional)
1 tsp vanilla extract
3 heaped tbsp cornflour (cornstarch)
1 x 375g (13oz) sheet of ready-rolled unsweetened shortcrust pastry*

1 lightly beaten egg* or a splash of milk*, to glaze

To decorate for baby
200g (1 cup) super-thick plain yogurt*
1 tbsp maple syrup (optional)
1 tsp alcohol-free vanilla extract

150g (5½oz) finely chopped strawberries

To decorate for big kids
100g (¾ cup) icing sugar
1–2 tbsp cold water
3 tbsp sprinkles

Preheat the oven to 200°C fan (220°C/425°F/Gas 7) and line a very large baking tray with non-stick baking paper or grease it with butter. Place a large dinner plate in the freezer to get cold.

Add the strawberries to a large bowl and mash with a fork. Alternatively, blitz them in a food processor, then transfer to a bowl. Add the maple syrup, if using, the vanilla extract and cornflour and mix well. Cover the bowl and cook the strawberries in the microwave on HIGH for 3 minutes.

Once the strawberry mixture is done, use a spatula to quickly spoon it onto the cold plate and spread it out in a flat layer. This will help it cool quickly.

While the filling cools, cut the pastry into 12 equal-size rectangles. Space six of the pastry rectangles out evenly on the prepared baking tray. Use a pastry brush to apply a small amount of beaten egg or milk to the outside edge of each piece of pastry, avoiding the centre.

Spoon a heaped tablespoon of the cooled strawberry mixture into the centre of each of the six pastry pieces. Take the remaining six pieces of pastry and sandwich them on top to make six tarts. Press the prongs of a fork around the edges of each tart to makes a pretty pattern and help seal the two pieces of pastry together. If the pastry is sticking to your fork, dip the fork in the beaten egg or milk and continue.

Brush each tart with beaten egg or milk, then pop the baking tray in the preheated oven for 15–20 minutes until golden all over and the pastry has puffed up a little. Remove from the oven and leave to cool on the tray.

Once cooled, top the pop tarts with thick yogurt mixed with maple syrup and vanilla extract, before sprinkling over the chopped strawberries. Or, for the big kids, mix the icing sugar and water together to make a paste. Spoon this icing onto each pop tart and add some sprinkles.

fruit bowl blender muffins

Empty your fruit bowl of soft fruit that is past its best for eating fresh and make these delicious little muffins. They're great for weaning and lunchboxes.

 GF*

 EF*

 V

 Vg*

 DF*

Makes 12 muffins

approx. 300g (10½oz) ripe fruit, e.g. bananas and apples
3 large eggs*
150g (⅔ cup) melted unsalted butter* or light olive oil

2 tsp vanilla extract
320g (scant 2½ cups) self-raising flour*
1 tsp baking powder*
50g (¼ cup) light soft brown sugar (optional)

extra fruit, to decorate, e.g. 1 banana (optional)
2 tsp demerara sugar, to finish (optional)

Prep 8 minutes, Bake 15–20 minutes

Preheat the oven to 180°C fan (200°C/400°F/Gas 6) and line a deep 12-hole muffin tin with non-stick paper cases.

Peel the fruit and remove any seeds or stones, if needed, and roughly chop. Add the chopped fruit to a large blender and whizz to a smooth purée.

Freezable

Add the eggs, melted butter or oil and vanilla extract and blend again to combine. Then add the dry ingredients and mix briefly until just combined. You want to avoid overworking the batter, so to be safe you can even mix this last bit by hand if you like. You're looking for a thick, dropping consistency, so if your fruit is particularly watery, you may need to add an extra tablespoon of flour to the batter.

♡

Love your leftovers

Leftovers will keep for up to 3–4 days in an airtight container, or freeze for up to 3 months. Defrost at room temperature, then enjoy cold or blast in the microwave at 20 second intervals on HIGH until they are soft and piping hot throughout.

Divide the mixture between the 12 muffin cases, filling them almost to the top. If you want to add a little decoration, thinly slice an extra piece of fruit and add a slice to the top of each muffin. Sprinkle a small pinch of demerara sugar on top of each muffin, if you like, as this will give a lovely golden and crisp finish.

Bake in the preheated oven for 15–20 minutes until the muffins are well risen, golden on top and an inserted knife comes out clean. Transfer to a wire rack to cool completely before enjoying. For little ones, remove the paper and cut the muffin into quarters or let them dig in whole if they can hold it well.

roasted garlic carrot sauce

 GF*

 EF

 V

 Vg*

 DF*

One of those recipes that's good to have up your sleeve. Carrots are inexpensive and fairly easy to grow in the garden, or so I'm told (not much of a gardener over here). This versatile sauce can coat your favourite pasta shapes, be easily transformed into a bowl of warming soup and/or be frozen into ice cube moulds to give to a young baby or use in soups and stews for an extra veggie hit. You could even defrost a few cubes and use them as a tomato-free pizza base topping, or with pitta breads or tortilla wraps for a speedy lunch.

Serves 2 adults and 2 littles, plus a bit extra

Prep 8 minutes, Cook 30 minutes

Freezable

Love your leftovers

To freeze the carrot purée, add it to ice cube trays and freeze for up to 3 months. Defrost at room temperature, then reheat until piping hot or cook from frozen in the microwave or in a pan until piping hot. The soup and the pasta sauce can also be frozen for up to 3 months. It's best to cook the pasta fresh.

6–8 large carrots (approx. 500g/ 1lb 2oz)
1 onion
2 tbsp garlic-infused oil
1 tsp dried thyme or dried mixed herbs
1 whole garlic bulb

Carrot purée variation
200ml (scant 1 cup) boiling water from the kettle

Pasta sauce variation
250ml (generous 1 cup) boiling water from the kettle
200g (7oz) dried pasta* (any shape you like), cooked according to the packet instructions
80g (2¾oz) smoked Cheddar cheese*, grated

Soup variation
400ml (1⅔ cups) boiling water from the kettle
1 low-salt vegetable or chicken stock cube*
100ml (scant ½ cup) single (light) cream*
freshly ground black pepper

Preheat the oven to 200°C fan (220°C/425°F/Gas 7) and line a very large baking tray with non-stick baking paper.

Peel the carrots and cut into chunks, around 4cm (1½in) long. Peel the onion and cut into quarter-wedges. Tip the onion and carrot onto the lined baking tray and drizzle with the garlic oil. Sprinkle over the herbs and toss well.

Cut the top off the garlic bulb, exposing the cloves inside. Nestle the garlic bulb, cut-side down, onto the tray between the veg. Ensure the ingredients are evenly spread with no overlapping, then roast in the preheated oven for 25–30 minutes, giving the carrots a toss halfway through cooking.

Add the roasted veg to a large saucepan or heatproof bowl. Place the roasted garlic on a chopping board and, using the back of a spoon, squeeze out as much soft roasted garlic as you can. Pick out the garlic skins and discard them, then add the roasted garlic to the carrots.

Add the correct amount of boiling water for the recipe variation you have chosen, then blend using a stick blender to a super-smooth purée.

To serve as a pasta sauce, add the cooked pasta and the grated cheese, stir well and serve. If you're making soup, crumble in the stock cube and bring to the boil. Add more water if you prefer a thinner soup, or boil for 5 minutes to thicken it. Serve with a drizzle of cream and a little black pepper.

crispy spiced cauliflower

 GF*

 EF*

 V

 Vg*

 DF*

I find if I jazz up everyday veg that my Nina would usually refuse, she's much more interested in wanting to try it – this one worked a treat!

Serves 2 adults and 2 littles

Prep 10 minutes, Bake 20 minutes

Freezable

Love your leftovers

Leftovers will keep in the fridge for up to 2 days. Reheat in the oven for 5 minutes until piping hot inside and crisp on the outside again. You can also freeze these for up to 3 months, reheating them in a hot oven from frozen for about 15 minutes until piping hot.

2 tbsp low-salt soy sauce*

2 tsp garlic granules

2 tsp mild curry powder

2 tsp dried mixed herbs

2 tsp smoked paprika

40g (generous ¼ cup) self-raising flour*

1 tsp baking powder*

2 eggs* (these can be replaced with an extra 120ml/½ cup of milk*)

70ml (⅓ cup) milk*

40g (⅓ cup) cornflour (cornstarch), plus 1 extra tbsp

9 tbsp panko breadcrumbs*

1 head of cauliflower, cut into florets

1–2 tsp garlic-infused oil

freshly ground black pepper

Preheat the oven to 200°C fan (220°C/425°F/Gas 7) and line a very large baking tray with strong, non-stick foil.

Add the soy sauce, garlic granules, curry powder, mixed herbs, paprika, flour, baking powder, eggs, milk, 40g (⅓ cup) of cornflour and 5 tablespoons of the panko breadcrumbs to a large bowl. Season with black pepper and mix well to combine into a batter.

Cut the florets of cauliflower into quarters, so they are bite-sized pieces. Sprinkle the extra tablespoon of cornflour over the cauliflower on the chopping board and toss in your hands to coat it well. Add the cauliflower to the bowl of batter and use a large spoon to toss and coat every floret evenly in the batter.

Sprinkle 1–2 tablespoons of the panko breadcrumbs over the baking tray, then lay the battered cauliflower florets out evenly on top, ensuring they aren't touching. If you happen to have excess batter in the bowl, avoid tipping it out onto the baking tray as it will take longer for the cauliflower to crisp up. Sprinkle the remaining panko breadcrumbs on top of the florets to help give a crispier finish, then drizzle with a little garlic oil. Bake in the preheated oven for 20 minutes, tossing halfway through. They are done once the veg is soft and the outside has turned golden brown.

Serve with cooked rice and your choice of dip (see pages 213–214). Or, try using the roasted cauli as a delicious taco or sandwich filling.

curried tuna fish cakes

Crisp on the outside and soft on the inside with a delicious, mild curry flavour, these simple fish cakes are perfect for lunch or dinner any day of the week. If you have any leftover cold mashed potato, this recipe is ideal for using it up.

Makes 6 large fish cakes

Prep 10 minutes, Bake 20–25 minutes

Freezable

Love your leftovers

These fish cakes will keep for up to 1–2 days in the fridge, but if you keep them they are best eaten cold to avoid reheating the tuna. You can also freeze these fish cakes, once they are shaped but not yet baked, for up to 3 months. Pop in the oven and bake for 30–35 minutes from frozen, until piping hot throughout.

2 tbsp garlic-infused oil
4 medium floury potatoes, such as Maris Piper or Russet
approx. 2 x 110g (3¾oz) cans of tuna in spring water, drained

60g (2oz) Cheddar cheese*, grated (optional)
2 tbsp low-salt soy sauce*
1 tsp mild curry powder
2 tsp garlic granules

1 medium egg*
1 heaped tbsp plain (all-purpose) flour*
approx. 4 tbsp panko breadcrumbs*
freshly ground black pepper

Preheat the oven to 200°C fan (220°C/425°F/Gas 7). Find a large baking tray, drizzle 1 tablespoon of the garlic oil evenly over the tray and set aside ready for later.

Peel the potatoes and thinly slice them into no more than 0.5cm (¼in) thick pieces. Add the sliced potatoes to a microwaveable bowl with a splash of water, cover and cook on HIGH for 3–4 minutes until tender. Drain the spuds, then add them to a cold bowl and mash with a potato masher. If you prefer, you can also cook the potatoes in a saucepan of boiling water for around 15 minutes until tender if you have extra prep time.

Meanwhile, add the tuna, cheese, soy sauce, curry powder, garlic granules, egg, flour and a little black pepper to a bowl and mix to combine. Add the mashed potatoes and mix well.

Add the panko breadcrumbs to the empty mash bowl. Divide the tuna mixture into six portions. Shape one portion into a rough patty shape, then drop it into the bowl of breadcrumbs. Turn the patty over to coat both sides in breadcrumbs and pat into shape again slightly, before transferring to the oiled baking tray. Repeat with the remaining tuna mixture to make six patties in total, then drizzle the remaining garlic oil over the fish cakes.

Pop the fish cakes in the preheated oven to bake for 20–25 minutes, flipping them over halfway through cooking, until golden and crisp on the outside. Alternatively, you can also fry the fish cakes in the oil in a non-stick frying pan for 5 minutes on each side until crisp and golden.

Serve with yogurt for dipping and a picky salad. Cut into finger strips to serve to little ones under 2.

pizza crackers

So quick to whip up, these crumbly little crackers taste like a cheesy tomato pizza – absolutely delicious! They're perfect for a picky snack plate or to pop in lunch boxes.

 GF*
 EF*
 V
 Vg*
 DF*

Makes approx. 40 crackers

160g (scant 1¼ cups) plain (all-purpose) flour*, plus extra for dusting
85g (⅓ cup) chilled unsalted butter*, cubed
100g (3½oz) Cheddar cheese*, grated
2 tsp dried porcini mushroom powder (optional)
2 tsp dried mixed herbs
2 tbsp tomato purée (paste)
1 medium egg*

Prep 10 minutes, Bake 8–10 minutes

Freezable

Love your leftovers

These crackers will keep for up to a week in an airtight container, or you can freeze the raw dough for up to 3 months. Defrost thoroughly, then roll out and bake as shown in method.

Preheat the oven to 190°C fan (210°C/415°F/Gas 6–7).

Add the flour and butter to a food processor and whizz until the mixture forms the texture of breadcrumbs. Add the cheese, dried porcini mushroom powder, if using, and dried herbs. Pulse until the ingredients are combined. Now add the tomato purée and egg, then whizz until the dough clumps together in the food processor.

Tip the ball of dough out onto a lightly floured work surface and tear it in two. Coat one of the pieces of dough in a little flour from the work surface, then use a rolling pin to quickly roll it out as thinly as you can. A thickness of around 3–4mm (⅛in) is fine – there is no need to be too neat as they will still turn out delicious.

Next, using a sharp knife, cut the dough into chunky strips. I'd suggest approx. 3cm (1¼in) wide and 5–6cm (2–2½in) long, but really any shape you like works. You can spend longer using cookie cutters to shape the crackers into pretty designs if you wish.

Space the crackers out on a large, non-stick baking tray, ensuring that they do not touch. If you have time or can be bothered, prick each cracker with a fork a few times to stop the crackers from puffing up too much.

I like to bake half when I make this recipe and freeze the rest of the dough for another day, so at this point you can either put the other half of dough in the freezer or roll it out and place the second lot of crackers on a second baking tray.

Bake in the preheated oven for 8–10 minutes until the crackers have darkened and puffed up a touch. Allow to stand on the tray for a minute or so to slightly firm up, then transfer to a wire rack to cool completely. Your kitchen will smell like a pizzeria, which is such an added bonus!

Serve as is in lunch boxes or with a picky plate (see page 216 for ideas) and your favourite dip (see pages 213–214).

green bean mini muffins

Green beans are a funny kind of vegetable that we only ever seem to boil and eat on their own or in a saucy dish. So, here's a lovely alternative use for that packet of green beans in your fridge. However, feel free to swap the green beans for canned sweetcorn or even some defrosted mixed veg from the freezer.

Makes 24 mini muffins

Prep 10 minutes, Bake 20 minutes

Freezable

Love your leftovers

Store leftovers in an airtight container in the fridge for up to 3 days, or freeze for up to 3 months. Defrost at room temperature and enjoy cold, or defrost and reheat in the microwave for around 2 minutes, checking halfway, until piping hot throughout.

200g (7oz) green beans
1 tsp dried porcini mushroom powder (optional)
1 tsp garlic granules
120g (scant 1 cup) self-raising flour*

1 tsp baking powder*
1 tsp mustard powder (optional)
100ml (scant ½ cup) milk*
2 medium eggs*

100g (3½oz) Cheddar cheese*, grated
a generous amount of freshly ground black pepper

Preheat the oven to 200°C fan (220°C/425°F/Gas 7) and place a silicone mini muffin mould onto a baking tray ready to fill. You can also use a non-stick metal muffin tin – just give it a spray with oil for good measure.

To trim the tips of your green beans quickly, take the unopened bag of green beans and find the side with most of the woody stems. Shake the bag so that all the woody stems fall to the same side and lie in the same position. Using a sharp knife, slice through all the green bean tips at once and then discard the packaging containing the tips.

Wash the beans, then slice them up as small as you can – the pieces should preferably be no bigger than 1cm (½in). Add the beans to a mixing bowl along with the rest of the ingredients, reserving a little grated cheese for sprinkling on top.

Briefly mix the batter with a tablespoon, then using another small spoon to help you, divide the batter into each mini muffin section of your tray.

Sprinkle the top of each muffin with a touch of the remaining cheese, then place the tray in the preheated oven to bake for 15–20 minutes, or until the muffins have puffed up and turned golden on top. Transfer to a wire rack and serve slightly warm, or leave to cool completely if storing for later.

Serve with a picky salad and a little yogurt to dip for a great lunch at home or on the go.

Add extra protein
Try mashing up ½ x 400g/14oz can of cooked (drained) chickpeas to add to the batter, or add a small drained can of tuna in spring water for a different take on these delicious little mouthfuls.

BATCH COOKING

No mini muffin tin?
If you don't have a
mini muffin mould or
tin, spoon the batter into
a well-greased regular
muffin tray and
bake for an extra
5–10 minutes.

Veggie swaps
Swap the cabbage for seasonal Brussels sprouts, grated or very finely chopped, for a new way to serve that 'love it or hate it' veggie.

sesame cabbage squares

 GF*

 EF*

 V

 Vg*

 DF*

If you have a cabbage dodger like my Nina, you've gotta make these. Grating the veg makes it super fine and it melts into these squares, which are flavoured with moreishly nutty sesame. These mouthfuls are a hit for lunch on the go or as a side for dinner.

Makes 12 squares

Prep 10 minutes, Bake 15–20 minutes

Freezable

Love your leftovers

These cabbage squares freeze well for up to 3 months. Store with greaseproof paper between each square so you can defrost only what you need. Either pop them in the toaster, or blast in the microwave for 60–90 seconds on HIGH until piping hot throughout. Or, store leftovers in an airtight container in the fridge for up to 3 days and enjoy cold or reheat as above.

140g (5oz) Savoy cabbage (approx. ½ head)

100g (3½oz) Cheddar cheese, grated*

1 tsp sesame oil (optional)

40g (generous ¼ cup) sesame seeds, plus extra for sprinkling on top

1 tbsp low-salt soy sauce*

100g (¾ cup) self-raising flour*

1 tsp baking powder*

2 large eggs*

120ml (½ cup) milk*

2 tsp garlic granules

Preheat the oven to 200°C fan (220°C/425°F/Gas 7). Line a medium baking tray, approx. 30 x 20cm (12 x 8in) in size, with non-stick baking paper.

Remove the coarse outer leaves of the cabbage, then grate it on the coarse side of a box grater.

Add the grated veg to a mixing bowl along with the rest of the ingredients. Stir well to combine them into a batter and pour the mixture into the prepared tin. Spread the batter out evenly to around 1.5cm (⅝in) in thickness, then scatter over a small amount of extra sesame seeds on top.

Bake in the preheated oven for 15–20 minutes, until risen and golden on top. Allow the bake to cool in the baking tray for a few minutes before removing using the paper and cutting it into 12 squares. Enjoy warm or cold.

If serving to little ones under 2, cut the squares into finger strips, which are easier for them to hold.

butternut squash oven-baked bhajis

 GF*

 EF

 V

 Vg*

 DF*

Packed with nutritious butternut squash, these little patties have a delicious, naturally sweet, soft interior which is mildly spiced with Indian flavours. They're great on their own as a snack, with a little salad for lunch or as a side for a main meal. They go deliciously with the Slow Cooker Beef Korma (see page 184).

Makes 12

Prep 10 minutes, Bake 30–35 minutes

Freezable

Love your leftovers

Leftovers will keep for up to 2-3 days in the fridge. These can also be stored for up to 1 day at room temperature, making them a great option for packed lunches. You can freeze them for up to 3 months. Reheat from frozen in an oven preheated to 180°C fan (200°C/400°F/ Gas 6) for 10-15 minutes, taking care to watch that they don't burn.

½ large butternut squash
120g (1⅓ cups) chickpea flour (gram flour) or plain (all-purpose) flour*
30g (¼ cup) cornflour (cornstarch)
1 tsp baking powder*

1 tsp ground turmeric
½ tsp ground coriander (optional)
1 tsp ground cumin
1 tsp garlic granules
2–3 tbsp garlic-infused oil, plus extra for greasing if needed

Cucumber yogurt dip
1 cucumber
200ml (1 cup) Greek yogurt*
freshly ground black pepper

Preheat the oven to 180°C fan (200°C/400°F/Gas 6).

Peel the butternut squash, remove any seeds or stringy bits and use the grater attachment on a food processor, if you have one, to coarsely grate it. You can also use the coarse side of a box grater, which may take a bit longer but is a good arm workout. You want to end up with approx. 450g (1lb) grated butternut squash.

Add the grated squash to a large bowl along with the chickpea or plain flour, cornflour, baking powder and spices. Stir well to coat every strand of the grated butternut squash with flour. Add 100ml (scant ½ cup) of cold tap water and stir. If the mixture feels dry still, add a splash more water.

Preferably use a silicone mould to prevent the bhajis from sticking, or liberally grease each indent of a non-stick 12-hole muffin tin with garlic oil. Add a spoonful of the bhaji mixture to each section. Pat the top of each portion down with the back of a spoon so that the batter fills the section. Drizzle the garlic oil over the top of each bhaji, then bake in the preheated oven for 30–35 minutes until the tops have turned golden.

While they bake, make a super simple cucumber yogurt dip by grating the cucumber on a box grater. Take the grated pulp in your hands and squeeze out a little of the juice over the sink, then transfer the grated cucumber to a bowl. Add the yogurt and a little black pepper and stir well.

Serve the warm bhajis with the cucumber yogurt dip on the side. Cut each bhaji in half for little ones under 2, so it's easier for them to hold.

No muffin tin?
You can also bake these on a flat baking tray instead of in a muffin tin – just use a spoon to shape the bhajis into 12 round circles. Try not to have any strands of butternut squash sticking out as these will catch easily.

cauliflower and broccoli crispy bakes

This recipe makes a big batch, but it won't be big enough I promise! These are so addictive, perfect for little ones who aren't sure on cauliflower as the flavour is mild and comforting. Everyone will love them.

Makes 20

Prep 10 minutes, Bake 25–30 minutes

Freezable

♡

Love your leftovers

These will store for up to 3 days in the fridge or freeze for up to 3 months. You can either freeze them uncooked and then cook them in the oven from frozen for around 35–40 minutes, or freeze them once baked and cooled, then reheat from frozen in the oven for around 10–15 minutes until piping hot inside.

400g (14oz) fresh cauliflower florets
200g (7oz) fresh broccoli florets
100g (3½oz) cornflour (cornstarch)
50g (generous ⅓ cup) self-raising flour*
2 large eggs*
100g (3½oz) Cheddar cheese*, grated
approx. 50g (generous 1 cup) panko breadcrumbs*
2 tbsp garlic-infused oil
freshly ground black pepper

Preheat the oven to 200°C fan (220°C/425°F/Gas 7). Find a large, shallow-sided baking tray and set it aside.

Add the cauliflower and broccoli florets to a food processor and whizz until they resemble very fine breadcrumbs (around 1–2 minutes of processing). Now, add the cornflour, self-raising flour, eggs, cheese and a little grinding of black pepper. Process again for 30 seconds, or until the ingredients are fully combined and you can't see any runny egg or white flour.

Pour the panko breadcrumbs into a small bowl and set aside. Take out a small amount of the cauliflower mixture, around the size of a golf ball, and briefly roll it into a ball between your palms. Add the veg ball to the bowl of breadcrumbs and swirl the bowl around, which will make the veg ball rotate, and the breadcrumbs stick to the outside. Flip it over, if needed, to make sure it is evenly coated in breadcrumbs all over, then place the ball on the baking tray. Slightly flatten with the palm of your hand to form a thick patty shape. Repeat the process with the rest of the mixture, you should get around 20 portions out of this recipe.

Drizzle the top of each patty with a little garlic oil, then pop the tray in the preheated oven for 25–30 minutes. I like to flip the bakes over halfway through cooking, which gives a crispier texture on both sides, but you don't have to so it's really up to you. They are done when the breadcrumbs have turned nice and golden on top.

Serve warm alongside salad or steamed veggies, with your carb of choice, or as part of a picky lunch. For little ones under 2, cut each crispy bake in half so it's easier for baby to pick up.

salmon rolls

Like a sausage roll, but made using canned salmon, beans and corn instead. Anything wrapped in puff pastry is delicious, right?! These little beauties are no exception.

 GF*

 EF*

 DF*

Makes 12 large salmon rolls

Prep 10 minutes, Bake 17–22 minutes

Freezable

Love your leftovers

These will keep for up to 2 days in an airtight container in the fridge. Alternatively, you can freeze them for up to 2 months. Either freeze before baking, then bake from frozen for around 30 minutes until piping hot, or freeze baked, cooled leftovers and reheat for 5–10 minutes from frozen until piping hot throughout.

150g (1 cup) drained and rinsed canned haricot beans
1 x 170g (6oz) can of salmon in spring water (no added salt)
165g (generous 1 cup) drained canned unsalted sweetcorn

60g (2oz) Cheddar cheese*, grated
1 tsp garlic purée
1 tsp smoked paprika
2 tbsp cream cheese* (optional)
1 x 375g (13oz) sheet of ready-rolled puff pastry*

1 egg*, whisked
1 tbsp sesame seeds or black onion seeds, to garnish

Preheat the oven to 200°C fan (220°C/425°F/Gas 7) and line a large baking sheet with non-stick baking paper.

Add the beans to a flat-bottomed bowl, reserving the rest of the can for another recipe such as Smoky Pork and Bean Stew (see page 164). Using a potato masher or the back of a large ladle, mash the beans to form a lumpy purée, then add the drained salmon, sweetcorn, grated cheese, garlic purée, smoked paprika and cream cheese. Mix well – it will feel like quite a firm mix, but it'll soften up once baked.

Unroll the puff pastry on a clean, flat work surface. Cut it in half lengthways so you have two long strips. Use two spoons to position half of the salmon mixture in a thin line across the length of each pastry sheet. There's no need to be too neat here, just make sure the salmon mixture reaches from edge to edge, and that it's not too thick or you may struggle to roll it up.

Brush the exposed pastry around the edges with the whisked egg. One at a time, roll each pastry strip up lengthways around the filling as tightly as you can, ensuring the ends overlap. Turn the rolls so the seam side is facing down, then cut each roll into 6 pieces. Transfer the salmon rolls to the lined baking sheet, placing them seam-side down again.

Brush the top of each salmon roll with more egg, then sprinkle with a few seeds before placing in the preheated oven to bake for 17–22 minutes, or until the pastry has puffed up, turned golden on top and the mixture is piping hot inside.

Leave to cool, then slice into finger strips to serve little ones, so it's easier for them to pick up and hold the rolls independently.

Note Some brands of canned salmon can be a little salty, so try to find ones with lower salt levels when shopping. Alternatively, swap the salmon for canned tuna, or use fresh cooked salmon instead.

savoury veg cake

This delightful cheesy bake will help get a few extra veggies in the kiddos. It's great for picnics, packed lunches and picky meals at home.

 GF*
 EF*
 V*
 Vg*
 DF*

Makes 10 generous slices

1 medium courgette (zucchini)
150g (5½oz) carrots, peeled
1 yellow pepper, deseeded and finely diced

85g (3oz) Emmental or Gruyère cheese*, finely grated, plus extra for sprinkling on top (optional)
200g (scant 1 cup) unsalted butter, softened*

4 medium eggs*
260g (2 cups) self-raising flour*
1 tsp baking powder*
60ml (¼ cup) milk*
a little freshly ground black pepper

Prep 10 minutes, Bake 30–40 minutes

Preheat the oven to 180°C fan (200°C/400°F/Gas 6) and grease and line a 20-22cm (8-8½in) round loose-bottomed cake tin with non-stick baking paper.

Coarsely grate the courgette and carrots using either a box grater or a food processor for speed. Add the grated veg to a clean tea towel, gather the sides in around the veg and twist the ends together over the sink to extract the juice – a lot should come out. Try and squeeze the ball of veg as tightly as you can to extract as much juice as possible, which will ensure you don't end up with a soggy cake. You should be left with approximately 230g (8oz) of the dry courgette and carrot mixture.

Freezable

Add the grated veg to the bowl of a stand mixer along with the remaining ingredients and whizz briefly for 20 seconds until just combined.

Pour the batter into the prepared cake tin and spread the top level. Sprinkle over a little more grated cheese, if you like, then pop the cake on the middle shelf of the preheated oven to bake for 30–40 minutes. Avoid opening the oven door before the 30-minute mark, as this may result in a sunken cake.

Love your leftovers

The cake will keep in an airtight container for up to 4 days at room temperature. You can also freeze wedges for up to 3 months. Wrap each one in non-stick baking paper and pop in an airtight container. When you would like to enjoy a slice, take a wedge out of the freezer, allow to defrost at room temperature and enjoy cold (great for packed lunches), or unwrap and microwave for 1–2 minutes, turning halfway through, until piping hot throughout.

You'll know the cake is done when it's well-risen with a golden top and a knife inserted comes out clean, although you may pull out a strand of melted cheese which is completely fine. Do note, the sponge may seem a little too moist when it's still warm as the cheese and veggies will still be soft; it will firm up as it cools. Leave the cake to cool in the tin for 10 minutes, then run a knife around the edge and turn it out onto a wire rack to cool for at least another 10 minutes. This cake is best served at room temperature, to allow the cheese to firm up.

Serve in wedges, or finger strips for little ones under 2, alongside a picky salad and yogurt for dipping, if desired.

Meat eater? Try adding a little chopped ham or cooked chicken to the batter before baking for extra protein.

spinach and pineapple mini muffins

These little mouthfuls are packed with nutrient-dense spinach, but you really wouldn't know it from the taste. Free from added sugar, they're great for packed lunches or grabbing a quick snack at home.

Makes 24 mini muffins

approx. 115g (4oz) frozen spinach or 4 shop-bought frozen blocks (see note)
1 ripe banana, peeled (roughly 100g/3½oz)

80ml (⅓ cup) milk*
2 medium eggs*
2 tsp vanilla extract
40ml (2⅔ tbsp) flavourless olive oil

150g (scant 1¼ cups) self-raising flour*
1 tsp baking powder*
1 x 400g (14oz) can of pineapple chunks in fruit juice, drained

Prep 10 minutes, Bake 20 minutes

Freezable

♡

Love your leftovers

These mini muffins will keep in an airtight container for up to 4 days at room temperature. You can also freeze them for up to 3 months. Just place one in the microwave from frozen and cook on HIGH for 60–90 seconds, or until defrosted and piping hot throughout. You can also allow them to defrost at room temperature and enjoy cold, which is a great option for lunch boxes.

Preheat the oven to 180°C fan (200°C/400°F/Gas 6) and grease a non-stick mini muffin tin or use a silicone mini muffin tray laid on top of a metal baking tray.

Add the frozen spinach, banana, milk, eggs, vanilla extract and oil to a blender and whizz until smooth.

Stir the self-raising flour and baking powder together in a mixing bowl. Pour the spinach mixture into the flour and fold together gently with a spatula. Be sure to stop mixing as soon as the flour is combined to avoid overworking the batter.

Divide the batter between each mini muffin section. Pop one chunk of pineapple into the centre of each mini muffin section on top of the batter and push down a little on it so that the batter nearly overflows at the sides (stopping just before this happens!).

Bake in the preheated oven for about 20 minutes or until the sponges have turned brown on the edges around the pineapple. Allow to cool for 10 minutes in the tin or tray before removing and serving to little ones, as the pineapple will be very hot.

If serving to little ones under 18 months, take the pineapple pieces out of the muffins and cut them in half or into quarters lengthways to reduce the size of the chunk just for safe measure. If the pineapple is very mushy, you don't need to do this.

Note You can use fresh spinach to make these muffins instead of frozen if you wish. Add approx. 200g (7oz) of fresh spinach leaves to a colander and place under the hot tap or pour over boiling water from the kettle to wilt it. Squeeze very well with the back of a ladle to remove as much water as possible. Add the spinach to the blender and continue as above.

fruity coconut macaroons

Soft and slightly chewy with a delicious nutty flavour, these coconut macaroons are much healthier than the traditional version.

 GF

 EF*

 V

 Vg*

 DF*

Makes 12

Prep 10 minutes, Bake 13–16 minutes

Freezable

Love your leftovers

Store in an airtight container for up to 3-4 days at room temperature or freeze for up to 3 months. If you plan to add chocolate to the macaroons, it's best to do this once they are defrosted as the chocolate will sweat in the defrosting process. Allow them to defrost at room temperature and enjoy cold.

1 ripe banana
2 tsp vanilla extract
1 x 90g (3¼oz) pouch of fruit purée (see tips on page 10)

200g (2⅔ cups) unsweetened desiccated (dried shredded) coconut
2 egg whites* or 4 tbsp aquafaba if EF

3 tbsp caster sugar (superfine in the US)
approx. 100g (3½oz) milk chocolate* (optional)

Preheat the oven to 170°C fan (190°C/375°F/Gas 5) and line a large baking tray with non-stick baking paper.

Peel the banana, place in a mixing bowl and mash it well with the back of a fork. Add the vanilla extract and fruit purée and stir. Add the coconut, mix well and set aside.

Separate the egg whites into a separate bowl and save the egg yolks for another recipe. Add the sugar to the egg whites, then use a large balloon whisk to beat the mixture for 2 minutes, until it has more than doubled in size and turned silky and white.

Add the egg whites to the coconut mixture and use a metal spoon to gently but confidently fold them together. It's important to avoid overworking the egg whites, so stop mixing as soon as you see it has combined well.

Use an ice-cream scoop to scoop out a heaped spoonful of the mixture, then deposit it onto the prepared baking tray. Using the ice-cream scoop will help you achieve a smooth domed top to the macaroons. You should get around 12 macaroons out of this mixture.

If there are any rogue pieces of coconut sticking up or on the baking tray, press them gently into the macaroons to avoid them catching and burning before the rest bakes.

Place the tray in the middle of your preheated oven and bake for 13–16 minutes, until the tops have turned golden all over. The change in colour is the main indication that they are cooked, as the macaroons will still feel very soft when they first come out of the oven. Allow them to cool completely and firm up on the tray or transfer to a wire rack.

These macaroons are delicious eaten as they are, but for an extra special touch for the big kids, melt a little milk chocolate and dip the base of each macaroon into the chocolate. Place them back on the non-stick baking paper, chocolate-side down to cool. The chocolate should take around 30 minutes to set. Once set, use a spatula to remove the macaroons from the baking paper and enjoy. Turn to the next page to see how they look.

An eggscellent tip
To successfully separate your eggs, the trick is to avoid breaking the egg yolk. Tap the egg on a flat surface instead of the thin edge of a bowl, which often causes sharp pieces of shell and can pierce the yolk. Then over a bowl, carefully prise the egg open into two halves. Pass the yolk back and forth between the two halves, as you do so the egg white should trickle out and into the bowl. Try to remove as much of the white as you can before setting the yolk aside in a separate bowl.

carrot cake soft-bake cookies

We do love a cookie, and even more so when there's a little hidden veg in there for the kiddos.

Makes 18 cookies

Prep 10 minutes, Bake 12–15 minutes

Freezable

Love your leftovers

Store these cookies in an airtight container at room temperature for up to 1 week. You can also freeze them for up to 3 months. Either allow to defrost at room temperature, or place on a baking sheet and bake from frozen for 5-10 minutes until defrosted and piping hot throughout.

120g (½ cup) unsalted butter, melted*
175g (6oz) carrot (roughly 1 large carrot), washed and coarsley grated
130g (1⅓ cups) rolled porridge oats*

150g (scant 1¼ cups) self-raising flour*
30–40g (⅛–scant ¼ cup) light soft brown sugar (optional)
1 x 90g (3¼oz) pouch of apple purée (see tips on page 10)

1 tsp mixed spice
2 tsp ground cinnamon
80g (½ cup) seedless raisins (optional)
1 large egg*

Preheat the oven to 180°C fan (200°C/400°F/Gas 6) and line one very large baking sheet or two medium baking sheets with non-stick baking paper.

Add all the ingredients to a mixing bowl and stir well. You want the egg to be fully distributed and the oats to soak up the moisture and spices.

Use a tablespoon to scoop out portions of mixture and mould them into little round mounds on the lined baking sheet, spacing them at least 5cm (2in) apart (you'll make about 18). Use the back of the spoon to smooth down any pieces of carrot that may be sticking up, otherwise these will burn in the oven.

Bake the cookies in the preheated oven for 12–15 minutes until golden on top. They will feel very soft when they first come out of the oven, but will firm up a little as they cool on the baking sheet.

almond custard twists

Light puff pastry, with a soft nutty custard filling. Chocolate chips are optional, but they add extra deliciousness to this low-sugar treat.

Makes 12

**Prep 10 minutes
Bake 14–18
minutes**

Freezable

**Love your
leftovers**

Leftovers will keep for up to 3 days in an airtight container, or freeze for up to 3 months. Defrost thoroughly before reheating for 5 minutes in a hot oven until crisp and piping hot again. You can also freeze the unbaked twists and cook them from frozen, adding an extra 5–10 minutes onto the bake time.

1 very ripe banana
50g (¼ cup) thick Greek yogurt*
1 tsp almond extract
1 tsp vanilla extract
120g (1¼ cups) ground almonds

1 medium egg*, plus extra for egg wash (optional)
1 tbsp maple syrup (optional)
1 x 375g (13oz) sheet of ready-rolled puff pastry*

scattering of chocolate chips* (optional)
1 tbsp icing (confectioners') sugar, to decorate (optional)

Preheat the oven to 200°C fan (220°C/425°F/Gas 7) and set a very large baking tray on the side ready to use.

Peel the banana, then mash with a fork in a medium bowl. Add the yogurt, almond extract and vanilla extract, ground almonds, egg and maple syrup, if using. Mix well with a fork, whisking the egg into everything else until you have a smooth paste.

Take the pastry out of the fridge and unroll it, leaving it on top of the paper it comes with. Work quickly now so that the pastry doesn't soften too much and make it harder to work with. Spread the almond filling evenly across the pastry using an offset spatula or the back of a spoon. Make sure it reaches right to the edges, so that the ends of the twists have plenty of filling too. Try and get an even layer, as any thicker areas of filling will become a little messy later. You can now sprinkle over some chocolate chips, if you wish.

Using the paper under the pastry to help you, fold the pastry in half lengthways, then peel back the paper from the top. With a large, sharp knife, cut the pastry sandwich into 12 strips, with a folded edge on each strip. I find it easiest to place the point of the knife at the top, where the pastry opens, then lever down the blade to slice through the pastry in one confident cut. This way you avoid lots of filling squishing out of the sides which may happen if you use a sawing motion.

Now hold each end of one pastry strip and quickly rotate your hands in opposite directions to twist the pastry, then place it on the baking tray. Repeat for the remaining pastry strips and space them evenly apart on the baking tray without touching. This may get a touch messy, but if you do the twists quickly, then the filling shouldn't come out too much.

If you wish, you can apply an egg wash to the exposed pastry to make it extra shiny, but it's not essential. Pop the baking tray in the centre of the preheated oven and bake for 14–18 minutes until the pastry is golden brown and flaky.

Remove from the oven and leave to cool a little. Dust the twists with icing sugar to add a touch more sweetness for the big kids, if you like, and serve.

apple loaf cake

Soft, moreish sponge with a crisp, sweet top, this cake has subtle hints of apple, cinnamon and gorgeous vanilla. It's perfect for an afternoon snack, lunch boxes or even breakfast!

 GF*

 EF*

 V

 Vg*

 DF*

Makes 10 slices of cake

Prep 10 minutes, Bake 45–55 minutes

Freezable

Love your leftovers

This cake keeps well for up to 4–5 days in an airtight container, or freeze for up to 4 months. If freezing, wrap individual slices in non-stick baking paper, then you can take one out at a time and it'll defrost in a few hours – perfect for lunchboxes!

2 red eating apples
200g (1½ cups) self-raising flour*
1 heaped tsp baking powder*
200g (generous ¾ cup) softened unsalted butter* OR 150ml (⅔ cup) sunflower oil
100ml (scant ½ cup) milk*
3 medium eggs*
80g (⅓ cup) golden caster sugar (superfine in the US)
2 tsp vanilla extract
2 tsp ground cinnamon

Topping
2 tbsp melted butter* or sunflower oil
1–2 tbsp golden caster sugar (superfine in the US), optional
2 tsp ground cinnamon

Preheat the oven to 170°C fan (190°C/375°F/Gas 5) and grease and line a 900g (2lb) loaf tin with non-stick baking paper.

Peel and grate the apples, discarding the cores. Add the grated apples and any escaping juices to a mixing bowl. Add the flour, baking powder, softened butter or oil, milk, eggs, sugar, vanilla extract and cinnamon. Mix briefly until the batter is smooth, taking care to avoid overmixing. Spoon the batter into the prepared tin and level out the top using the back of a spoon.

For the topping, combine the melted butter or oil, sugar, if using, and cinnamon in a small bowl. Mix well, then drizzle this over the top of the cake batter. Using a teaspoon, very roughly swirl the cinnamon mixture into the batter. Avoid mixing it in completely, you just want to distribute the ingredients around the top of the cake a little more.

Pop the tin in the centre of the preheated oven and bake for 45–55 minutes, or until a skewer inserted comes out clean. Check the cake after 35 minutes, if the top is burning or browning too quickly while the middle still looks wobbly, then cover the tin with a little foil hat, this will stop the top burning by the time the cake is cooked in the middle.

Once baked, allow the cake to cool in the tin for 10 minutes, before removing and transferring to a wire rack to cool further. You can enjoy this cake slightly warm, or it's equally delicious cold.

Note This cake is already very low in sugar, but feel free to reduce the amount or leave it out entirely if serving to under 1's in particular.

nutty carrot bars

 GF*

 EF*

 V

 Vg*

 DF*

These low-sugar cake bars are healthier than your average shop-bought sweet treat. They're packed with veg and made with nutritious almonds for added flavour and texture.

Makes 12 bars

Prep 10 minutes, Bake 20–25 minutes

Freezable

Love your leftovers

These cake bars will keep for up to a week in an airtight container at room temperature, or portions wrapped in non-stick baking paper will freeze for up to 3 months. Defrost at room temperature for a few hours before enjoying.

250g (9oz) carrot, peeled and finely grated
50g (⅓ cup) almond flour
150g (scant 1¼ cups) self-raising flour*
1 tsp baking powder*

50g (¼ cup) almond butter (or use any nut butter or sunflower seed butter)
2 medium eggs*
50–80g (¼–⅓ cup) light soft brown sugar (optional)
2 tsp vanilla extract

1 tsp almond extract
100g (scant ½ cup) unsalted butter*, well softened
handful of shelled walnuts, chocolate chips* or fruit, for the topping (optional)

Preheat the oven to 180°C fan (200°C/400°F/Gas 6) and line a 20cm (8in) square brownie tin with non-stick baking paper.

Add the grated carrots to the bowl of your stand mixer, along with any escaped carrot juices. Add all the remaining ingredients, apart from the walnuts/chocolate chips/fruit. Mix briefly, stopping just as the batter comes together to avoid overworking it.

Spoon the batter into your prepared cake tin, spread it out right to the edges and level the top. The batter will feel a little firm, but this is okay because as the carrots cook they will steam and make the sponge moist.

My favourite topping for these cake bars is halved walnuts, as they toast a little in the oven and bring a wonderful texture. However, it is important to avoid serving large pieces of nuts to children under 5, so to get around this you can crush the walnuts, using a knife, food processor or in a pestle and mortar. Ensure there are no pieces larger than 0.5cm (¼in), then sprinkle the crushed nuts on top. You could do half the cake with halved nuts and the other side topped with crushed nuts to cater for the whole family if you'd like. Alternatively, keep the nuts as they are and remove before giving the cake bars to your little ones. You can also opt for chocolate chips or a fruit without too much moisture, like thinly sliced apple.

Bake in the preheated oven for 20–25 minutes until the cake has risen well, the top is golden and a knife inserted comes out clean. Allow to cool for 5 minutes in the tin before removing from the tin and slicing into 12 bars. If you have used halved walnuts, you may find it easier to wait until the cake is cold to cut to avoid the walnuts mashing into the sponge.

nutty oat cookies

Soft, small nutty morsels, perfectly sized for little fingers – if the big kids leave any for them that is!

 GF*

 EF

 V

 Vg*

 DF*

Makes 20 small cookies

Prep 10 minutes, Bake 12–14 minutes

Freezable

Love your leftovers

Store the cookies in an airtight container for up to a week, or freeze them for up to 3 months. They can be defrosted at room temperature and enjoyed cold, or pop a frozen cookie on a tray in a hot oven and bake for 5–10 minutes until piping hot throughout.

2 ripe bananas (approx. 170g/6oz)
150g (1½ cups) rolled porridge oats*
75g (2½oz) finely chopped nuts, or ground almonds if serving to little ones under 1
1 tsp almond extract
20–30g (1½–2½ tbsp) light soft brown sugar (optional)
1 tbsp golden syrup or honey* for over 1s (optional)
½ tsp baking powder*
100g (scant ½ cup) unsalted butter*, softened or melted
85g (⅔ cup) plain (all-purpose) flour*

Preheat the oven to 180°C fan (200°C/400°F/Gas 6) and line a large baking tray with non-stick baking paper.

Mash the bananas in a large bowl, then add all the remaining ingredients and stir well to combine.

Scoop out heaped tablespoons of the mixture and gently form them into circle shapes on the prepared baking tray. Try to space the rounds of dough evenly apart so they're not touching. You should get around 20 cookies out of this mixture.

Flatten each cookie dough round using the tips of your fingers until they are around 1cm (½in) in thickness. There's no need to be neat, the indents your fingers make and any rustic edges will give delicious colour and flavour to the finished cookies.

Place the tray in the centre of the preheated oven and bake the cookies for 12–14 minutes or until the edges have started to turn golden. They will feel quite soft when you initially remove them from the oven, but they should firm up as they cool.

strawberry orange cake squares

The addition of cream cheese in the cake batter not only gives a delicious flavour, but also makes the texture slightly dense, giving these little cake squares a luxurious, comforting feel.

 GF*
 EF*
 V
 Vg*
 DF*

Makes 16 small squares

Prep 10 minutes, Bake 30–40 minutes

Freezable

Love your leftovers

This cake will keep for up to 3–4 days in an airtight container at room temperature, or freeze for up to 3 months. Allow to defrost at room temperature and enjoy.

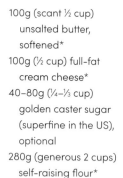

100g (scant ½ cup) unsalted butter, softened*

100g (½ cup) full-fat cream cheese*

40–80g (¼–⅓ cup) golden caster sugar (superfine in the US), optional

280g (generous 2 cups) self-raising flour*

1 tsp baking powder*

grated zest of 1 orange

2 tsp vanilla extract

3 large eggs*

1 x 90g (3¼oz) fruit purée pouch (see tips on page 10) OR 1 large ripe banana, mashed

200g (7oz) strawberries, leaves removed and thinly sliced

1 heaped tsp icing (confectioners') sugar, to decorate (optional)

Preheat the oven to 180°C fan (200°C/400°F/Gas 6). Grease the sides of a 20cm (8in) square cake tin and line the base with non-stick baking paper.

Add the softened butter, cream cheese and sugar, if using, to a stand mixer and mix until they are well combined. Weigh in all the remaining ingredients, apart from the strawberries and icing sugar. Mix until well combined, stopping as soon as you can't see lumps of any ingredient to avoid overworking the batter.

Pour the batter into the prepared cake tin and level the top, making sure the batter reaches into all the corners. Arrange the sliced strawberries over the top of the batter. Pop the cake into the preheated oven to bake for 30–40 minutes, until the batter is golden on top and a knife inserted comes out clean. Avoid opening the oven door before the 25-minute mark to ensure the cake doesn't sink.

Allow the cake to cool in the tin for 5 minutes before removing and placing on a board or serving plate. Dust the top with the icing sugar, if you wish. As this cake is very low in sugar already, the tiny dusting of sugar on top does help remind us that it is a sweet treat. If you have kept the sugar in the batter to a minimum for serving to little babas, add a touch more icing sugar on top of the adult portions to help balance the sweetness. Cut into 16 squares for serving.

banana puffs

Naturally sweet banana discs wrapped in a vanilla and cinnamon flaky pastry swirl, these sweet little mouthfuls are super easy to make with minimal ingredients.

 GF*
 EF*
 V
 Vg*
 DF*

Makes 12–14 puffs

Prep 10 minutes, Bake 15–20 minutes

Freezable

Love your leftovers

Store the banana puffs in an airtight container at room temperature for up to 3 days, or freeze for up to 3 months. To defrost, place in a hot oven from frozen for 10–12 minutes until piping hot, but be careful to watch they don't burn.

1 x 375g (13oz) sheet of ready-rolled puff pastry*
3 large ripe bananas, peeled
1 tbsp vanilla extract
1 tbsp maple syrup (optional)
1 medium egg*, beaten
2 tsp ground cinnamon,
plus a little extra for sprinkling
2 tsp demerara sugar (optional)

Preheat the oven to 200°C fan (220°C/425°F/Gas 7) and line a large baking sheet with non-stick baking paper.

Unroll the pastry and lay it out horizontally in front of you on a flat, clean work surface.

Work quickly here as the pastry will become sticky and difficult to work with if sat out for too long. Mash half of one of the bananas with a fork in a small bowl. Add the vanilla extract, maple syrup, if using, and 2 tablespoons of the beaten egg. Mix very well, then scrape every last bit onto the pastry. Use the back of a spoon or a pastry brush to spread the mixture evenly across, reaching right to the edges of the pastry. Use your fingertips to sprinkle the cinnamon over from a height so there is an even coating.

Place the remaining 2½ bananas in a line across the length of the pastry sheet, positioned approx 7.5cm (3in) away from the edge closest to you. You essentially want a long sausage shape, with no gaps between the bananas if possible. If your bananas are a little bendy, tear them in half to straighten the sausage shape out. Gather the pastry edge closest to you and roll the pastry up and around the bananas. Keep rolling up until all the pastry is wrapped around the fruit.

Trim the ends of the pastry if there's no banana inside, then cut into 2cm (¾in) discs using a sharp knife. Lay the discs on the lined baking sheet, cut banana-side up. If any banana pieces fall out, just push them back into the centre of the pastry. The pastries may look a little messy right now, but don't worry as they'll puff up and even out as they bake.

Brush the remaining beaten egg over the sides and top of each banana puff. Sprinkle a tiny amount of extra cinnamon on each banana piece. If you like, add a tiny sprinkling of demerara sugar to each one too, this will caramelize in the oven to give a delicious taste and texture.

Bake in the preheated oven for 15–20 minutes until the pastry has puffed up and turned golden on top. Allow to cool on the tray for 10 minutes before serving warm, or let cool completely and store to enjoy cold later on.

one-pan wonders

This is simple cooking, using just one pan or tray for the whole meal to make your time in the kitchen feel fuss-free and oh-so-much-more enjoyable. There's something so lovely about letting all those flavours mingle together as they cook side by side resulting in a comforting, delicious dish. And, for me, it's all about the minimal washing up!

chicken and rice soup

A fab way to use up leftover chicken from your Sunday roast. With protein, veg and carbs in one bowl, this delicious meal will warm you up on a cold day.

 GF*

 EF

 DF

Serves 2 adults and 2 littles

Prep 8 minutes, Cook 12–15 minutes

Freezable

Love your leftovers

Cool the soup as quickly as possible and store in an airtight container in the fridge for up to 2 days or in the freezer for up to 3 months. Defrost thoroughly in the fridge before reheating in a saucepan until bubbling and piping hot throughout.

1 tbsp garlic-infused oil
2 spring onions (scallions) OR 1 small white onion
approx. 225g (8oz) carrots
1 garlic clove, crushed

2 low-salt chicken stock cubes*
120g (⅔ cup) long- or short-grain white rice
approx. 250g (9oz) cooked shredded chicken

freshly ground black pepper
2 tbsp fresh chopped parsley, to serve (optional)

Add the garlic oil to a large saucepan over a medium-high heat and let it heat up. Meanwhile, boil the kettle and thinly slice the spring onions or dice the onion. Add the onion to the pan and sauté for 1–2 minutes until softened. While the onion is cooking, peel and finely chop or grate the carrots.

Add the garlic and carrots to the saucepan and cook for 30 seconds while you measure out 1.3 litres (5½ cups) of boiling water from the kettle into a large measuring jug. Add the crumbled stock cubes and stir well to dissolve them in the water. Add the hot chicken stock to the saucepan, followed by a generous grinding of black pepper.

Measure the rice into a sieve and wash it under cold running water, using your fingers to ensure the grains are very clean, for 1 minute or until the water runs clear. This stops the soup from becoming too starchy.

Add the wet rice to the saucepan along with the cooked shredded chicken. Allow the soup to come up to a gentle rolling boil and cook for around 12 minutes, until the rice and carrots are fully cooked and tender.

Top the soup up with a little more boiling water out of the kettle if you would like a thinner consistency, then serve up into bowls with a little sprinkling of chopped parsley, if you like. Adults, you may enjoy a sprinkling of salt on your portion.

If you are serving to little ones who haven't mastered using a spoon yet, strain the broth from the soup and serve it separately in an open cup or a free flowing sippy cup with the rice and veggies on the side. If you have opted for chopped carrots, be sure to mash any larger pieces with a fork for little ones under 3.

easy oven-baked crisps

This method of making crisps is healthier and safer than deep-frying potatoes. It's also great for all the family because there will be some crisps which are deliciously crunchy and some with moreish, soft edges, perfect for little taste testers – if the older kids let them have any!

 GF

 EF

 V

 Vg

DF

2–3 large white all-rounder potatoes

1–2 tbsp sunflower oil

Makes a generous bowl of crisps to share

Prep 10 minutes, Bake 25–30 minutes

Love your leftovers

These crisps are best served straight away, but they will keep in an airtight container at room temperature for a day or two. For best results, pop back in a hot oven for 5 minutes to warm through before serving.

Preheat the oven to 200°C fan (220°C/425°F/Gas 7) and line one large or two medium baking trays with non-stick foil, (it's particularly important you use the non-stick variety of foil for this recipe) or non-stick baking paper.

Wash your potatoes well and give them a dry.

Using the slicing side of a box grater or a mandolin, slice the potatoes with the skin still on. If using a box grater, hold the potato with a clean tea towel as it reaches the end to save your fingers, and definitely use a guard if slicing on a mandolin. I prefer using the box grater because you get irregular widths, meaning there's some crispier bits and some softer bits, which I find delicious!

Working quickly to avoid the potatoes browning, spread the slices onto your baking tray, then drizzle over the sunflower oil. Toss the potatoes in the oil, then spread them out as evenly as you can to avoid any layering, as any potato underneath will steam and stay very, very soft instead of turning crisp.

Place in the preheated oven near the hottest heat source and bake for 25–30 minutes, or until the potatoes are turning golden.

For adults and older kids, add a sprinkling of salt and black pepper to serve. For an option to suit younger babies too, try adding a pinch of smoked paprika before or after baking. Serve with low-salt and low-sugar tomato ketchup or a selection of dips (see pages 213–214).

easy one-pan meatloaf kebab

The idea of cooking a kebab might feel like it involves a lot of work, but this one is as simple as they come. You can serve the meat however you like, with some oven-baked potatoes is delicious. Nina and I particularly love to stuff the meat into wraps or pittas with some nice salad and a dip for a picky style family meal. Plus, this is a fantastic way to serve soft meat to baby as you can control what shape it'll be for little fingers to hold.

 GF*

 EF*

 DF

Serves 2 adults and 2 littles

500g (1lb 2oz) minced (ground) pork or lamb (15–20% fat)
2 tsp garlic paste
2 tsp onion granules
2 tsp smoked paprika
2 tsp ground cumin
2 tsp dried mixed herbs
2 tbsp breadcrumbs*
1 medium egg* (optional)
2 tsp garlic-infused oil
1 tbsp sesame seeds
freshly ground black pepper

Prep 10 minutes, Bake 20 minutes

Freezable

Love your leftovers

Leftovers will keep for up to 3 days in the fridge or freeze for up to 3 months. You can freeze the kebab once it has baked and then defrost it in the fridge before reheating for approx. 5–10 minutes in the oven until piping hot. Or make a double batch, freeze the raw spare in a disposable foil tray and bake for an extra 10 minutes or so from frozen until piping hot.

Preheat the oven to 230°C fan (250°C/485°F/Gas 9½), or as hot as it will go.

Place a stoneware or non-stick metal oven dish on the side ready to use. Ideally the dish should be around 20 x 30cm (8 x 12in) in size, but a little smaller or larger will work too. Ensure the sides of the dish aren't too high, as this will stop the kebab from colouring nicely.

Leave the meat in its open packet or transfer it to a bowl and add the garlic paste, onion granules, spices, herbs, breadcrumbs, egg, if using, and a generous grinding of black pepper. Using your hand, mix really well, squishing the meat in your fist to help it combine with the other ingredients.

Transfer the meat to the oven dish and spread it out into an even, flat layer, around 2cm (¾in) in thickness. There's no need to get the ruler out, just try to keep it as even as possible. Drizzle the garlic oil over, then sprinkle the sesame seeds on top of the meat, these will toast and give a lovely colour.

Bake in the preheated oven for 15–20 minutes, or until the top of the meat has turned golden. To serve, cut into strips for the little ones to pick up and hold, or into 6 squares to stuff inside a pitta bread or a flatbread. Delicious served with a little salad and yogurt.

Try my Japanese Smacked Cucumber Pickle (see page 215) or a home-made dip (see pages 213–214) as your accompaniments.

creamy tuna and tomato gnocchi

The sauce in this comforting meal is a cross between a classic tomato sauce and a thick, creamy white cheese sauce, making it deliciously oozy and decadent.

Serves 2 adults and 2 littles

Prep and cook 10 minutes

Freezable

Love your leftovers

This will keep for up to 2 days in the fridge or up to 3 months in the freezer. Defrost, then reheat in the oven until piping hot throughout, adding a touch of water to help loosen the sauce if it's looking a little dry.

30g (2 tbsp) unsalted butter*
2 level tsp cornflour (cornstarch)
300ml (1¼ cups) milk*
500g (1lb 2oz) passata (strained tomatoes)

3 large handfuls of frozen peas
500g (1lb 2oz) fresh gnocchi*
1 low-salt chicken or vegetable stock cube*
1 tsp smoked paprika

2 x approx. 110g (3¾oz) cans of tuna in spring water*, drained
100g (3½oz) Cheddar cheese*, grated
freshly ground black pepper

Bring a saucepan of water to the boil, using boiling water from the kettle to speed the process up.

Meanwhile, add the butter to a large, non-stick frying pan over a high heat and allow it to melt. Add the cornflour and stir into the melted butter.

Gradually pour in the milk with one hand, whisking continuously with the other hand to help the sauce come together and remove any lumps. Next, add the tomato passata gradually and whisk in. The sauce should be starting to thicken up nicely now.

Add the peas to the boiling water in your saucepan, then the gnocchi and cook according to the packet instructions. The peas will take 4 minutes to boil, so don't add the gnocchi until the peas are nearly done if it's fresh and doesn't need long.

Back to the sauce. Crumble in the stock cube, then add the smoked paprika, drained tuna, Cheddar cheese and a generous grind of black pepper. Give everything a good stir until well combined.

When the gnocchi and peas are cooked, drain and mix them with the sauce in the pan to serve.

If you have an extra 20 minutes, pour the finished gnocchi into an oven dish, top with more cheese and bake in a preheated oven at 200°C fan (220°C/425°F/Gas 7) until crispy on top – it's utterly delicious!

Veggie swaps Swap the tuna for canned unsalted sweetcorn, chickpeas or lentils for a protein-rich vegetarian alternative.

panko wings and crispy spuds

Crunchy on the outside and soft in the middle, with the irresistible flavour combo of lemon and garlic – these wings are utter heaven, the whole fam will love them!

Serves 2 adults and 2 littles as part of a meal

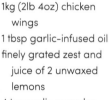

1kg (2lb 4oz) chicken wings
1 tbsp garlic-infused oil
finely grated zest and juice of 2 unwaxed lemons
4 tsp garlic granules OR 2 large garlic cloves, crushed

1 tsp dried mixed herbs
approx. 60g (1⅓ cups) panko breadcrumbs*
garlic-infused oil spray
freshly ground black pepper

Crispy spuds
approx. 300-400g (10½-14oz) new potatoes, washed
1 tbsp garlic-infused oil

Prep 10 minutes, Bake 30 minutes

Freezable

Love your leftovers

If you can, keep a couple of wings for tomorrow – they are delicious cold. Leftovers will keep for up 2 days in the fridge, or freeze for up to 3 months. Defrost, then reheat in the oven for 5–10 minutes until piping hot throughout.

Preheat the oven to 200°C fan (220°C/425°F/Gas 7) and line a very large baking tray with non-stick foil. (If you don't have a baking tray big enough to fit the wings and spuds on together, you can use 2 smaller trays instead).

Add the chicken wings to a large bowl or a sealable food bag (or leave them in the packet they came in to save washing up), then add the garlic oil, lemon zest and juice, the garlic granules or fresh garlic, dried herbs and a good grinding of black pepper and mix well. Now, add 5 heaped tablespoons of the panko breadcrumbs to the wings and toss to coat them in the marinade – the breadcrumbs will soften and soak up the marinade, don't worry, this is good.

Scatter the wings onto one half of the prepared baking tray and space them evenly apart so they don't overlap. Ensure each wing is skin-side up. If there are any clumps of marinade-soaked breadcrumbs left behind, spoon them out and place a little on any wings that look a little bare. Now sprinkle an extra tablespoon of panko breadcrumbs onto each wing, adding a little less for smaller wings or a touch more for any large wings. Squirt about 4 sprays of garlic-infused oil spray onto each wing, the breadcrumbs will soak up some of the oil, which will help them crisp up. If you don't have a spray bottle, just try to evenly sprinkle and drizzle a little garlic oil over each wing instead.

For the crispy spuds, thinly slice the new potatoes with a knife, approx 0.5cm (¼in) in thickness. Scatter the potato slices over the other half of the baking tray (or a second tray, if needed). Drizzle with the garlic oil, then place everything (wings and potatoes) in the preheated oven and bake for about 30 minutes, or until the breadcrumbs on the wings are golden and the chicken is cooked through.

Use a firm fish slice to scoop each wing up off the foil. P.S. Those crispy bits stuck on the tray are the best bit! Serve with the crispy spuds and salad. Remove the meat and skin from the wings for little taste testers if you like.

one-pot satay aubergine rice

Warming and comforting, this one-pot wonder is great to whip up on busy midweek evenings.

Serves 2 adults and 2 littles

Prep 10 minutes, Cook 15–20 minutes

Freezable

Love your leftovers

Leftovers will keep in the fridge for up to 24 hours, but you need to cool the rice down quickly to ensure it's safe to eat. To do this, spread leftovers over a cold plate, then as soon as they're cold, place in an airtight container in the fridge. This dish can also be kept, frozen, for up to 1 month. Defrost in the fridge, then reheat in a saucepan with a splash of water, or cover and microwave for 2–3 minutes until piping hot throughout.

1 tbsp garlic-infused oil
1 large or 2 small aubergines (eggplants)
250g (1⅓ cups) long-grain rice
1 x 400g (14oz) can of coconut milk

1 low-salt vegetable or chicken stock cube*
2 tbsp low-salt soy sauce*
3 heaped tbsp smooth peanut butter (100% nuts)

2 tsp mild curry powder
2 tsp garlic granules
1 tbsp toasted sesame seeds, to garnish (optional)

Set a large saucepan, preferably non-stick, over a medium-high heat. Add the garlic oil and let it heat up.

Cut the aubergine into 1cm (½in) cubes. Add the aubergine to the saucepan and stir well. Pop the lid on and cook for around 5–7 minutes, stirring often, until it's turning soft and gaining a lovely golden colour. Remember to cover the pan with the lid again after each stir, as the steam helps the aubergine cook. Add a splash of water to the pan if you feel it's sticking too much.

Meanwhile, wash the rice in a sieve under cold running water until the water runs clear, then set aside until needed.

Once the aubergine is soft, add the coconut milk to the pan to stop the aubergine frying. Crumble in the stock cube, then add the soy sauce, peanut butter, curry powder, garlic granules and the washed rice and stir very well. When the contents of the pan are bubbling at the edges, pop the lid on tightly and allow to cook over a medium heat for 12–17 minutes.

Avoid taking the lid off to check it before the 12-minute mark. If it still looks very sticky when you do check, place the lid back on and cook for a further few minutes. Take the pan off the heat with the lid still on and allow the dish to stand, covered, for at least 5–10 minutes to let the rice soak up more of the flavours.

Serve as is, or with a little extra veg on the side and a sprinkling of toasted sesame seeds to garnish, if you like. Adults, you may like to season your portion a little more for this one.

spiced salmon and veggie tray bake

This one-tray bake is so quick, easy and delicious. Try it without the salmon if you'd like to keep it veggie, or swap the fish for chickpeas or firm tofu for a meat-free protein option.

 GF

 EF

 V*

 DF

Serves 2 adults and 2 littles

Prep 10 minutes, Bake 25–30 minutes

♡

Love your leftovers

Leftovers will keep for up to 24 hours in the fridge. Reheat in the oven for 5–7 minutes, or until piping hot throughout. Bear in mind that salmon can easily overcook and become dry, so try not to heat it up for too long.

300g (10½oz) medium-large new potatoes, quartered lengthways
1 aubergine (eggplant), cut into batons
1 large courgette (zucchini), cut into batons
1 red pepper, deseeded and cut into strips
1 red onion, root left intact but cut into wedges
3–4 large salmon fillets*

Marinade
3 tbsp garlic-infused oil
2 tsp dried mixed herbs
2 tsp smoked paprika
2 tsp garlic granules
juice of 1 lemon
2 tsp mild curry powder
1 tbsp cornflour (cornstarch)
a little freshly ground black pepper

Preheat the oven to 190°C fan (210°C/415°F/Gas 6–7) and line a very large baking tray with non-stick foil.

Place the quartered new potatoes and aubergine batons into a microwaveable bowl. Add approx. 150ml (⅔ cup) of cold water from the tap (you don't have to measure this out, really it's just a good splash at the bottom of the bowl). Cover and microwave on HIGH for 5 minutes.

Meanwhile, make up the marinade. Combine all the ingredients in a large mixing bowl and stir well. Add the courgette batons, chopped pepper and onion wedges. Once the potatoes and aubergine are done, drain and add them to the marinade bowl too. Use a large spoon to toss the veggies around to coat them in the marinade.

Tip everything out onto the prepared baking tray, making sure you leave any excess marinade in the bowl. Spread the veggies flat and pop the tray in the preheated oven for 15 minutes.

Now, quickly add the salmon fillets to the marinade bowl and move them around so that they soak up all the flavour all over. Leave to stand in the marinade while the veggies bake.

After 15 minutes, pull the tray out of the oven and give the veggies a quick toss before nestling the salmon fillets into the centre of the vegetables. Pop the tray back into the oven for a further 12–15 minutes, or until the salmon is cooked through. To check this, gently pull a flake away from the fattest part of a fillet, if it comes away easily and the colour is pale pink throughout, it's ready to eat.

Serve the salmon flaked slightly for little fingers. Adults can have theirs with a tiny sprinkling of salt.

You can see me holding the full tray bake on the front cover of this book.

fajita no-boil pasta bake

This throw-it-all-in pasta bake is the type of recipe you want when you haven't got much time to cook. It's comforting, creamy, flavourful and delicious.

Serves 2 adults and 3 littles

Prep 10 minutes, Bake 1 hour

Freezable

Love your leftovers

Leftovers will keep for up to 2-3 days, tightly covered, in the fridge. Add a splash of water over the pasta and bake, uncovered, at 180°C fan (200°C/400°F/Gas 6) for around 15 minutes until piping hot throughout. You can also freeze leftovers for up to 3 months – add more water as above and bake from frozen for around 20–25 minutes until fully defrosted and piping hot throughout. Stir halfway to help it along.

2 low-salt chicken or vegetable stock cubes*
500g (1lb 2oz) boneless skinless chicken breasts or thighs*, cut into strips or diced
1 red pepper, deseeded and sliced
1 yellow pepper, deseeded and sliced

2 tsp garlic granules
2 heaped tsp smoked paprika
1 tsp ground cumin
1 tsp ground coriander
350ml (1½ cups) milk*
500g (1lb 2oz) tomato passata (strained tomatoes)
240g (2¾ cups) dried penne pasta*

120g (4½oz) Cheddar cheese*, grated
freshly ground black pepper

To serve (optional)
guacamole
sour cream*
lime wedges

Preheat the oven to 180°C fan (200°C/400°F/Gas 6) and boil the kettle.

Crumble the stock cubes into a measuring jug, then add 100ml (scant ½ cup) of boiling water from the kettle. Stir well, then leave for a minute or so before stirring again to allow the stock cubes to dissolve into a thick paste.

Meanwhile, add the chicken, peppers, garlic granules and all the herbs and spices to a large, high-sided baking dish (approx. 25 x 35cm/10 x 14in).

Back to the stock in the jug, add the milk and stir to dissolve the stock paste before pouring this liquid into the baking dish. Stir well, then add the tomato passata, the pasta and half of the grated cheese. Stir again – as the dish is quite full it may be useful to use two wooden spoons to lift the ingredients and help mix them together until they are well combined. Ensure all the ingredients are submerged under the liquid, then cover the dish tightly with foil. Place on the middle shelf of the preheated oven and forget about it for 40 minutes – it will bubble away and cook on its own.

After 40 minutes, carefully check the pasta. If it's soft, remove the foil and give it all a good stir. If it's not, then re-cover and cook for a while longer. Top with the remaining grated cheese and a little black pepper. Turn the oven temperature up to 200°C fan (220°C/425°F/Gas 7) and place the uncovered dish back in the oven. Bake for a further 10–15 minutes, until the cheese has melted and the top of the pasta bake is beginning to char.

Serve with guacamole, sour cream, lime wedges and a sprinkle of salt for the adults. For little taste testers, cut the chicken into finger strips or blend up baby's portion with a little milk or water.

Veggie swaps Replace the chicken with diced aubergines (eggplants) and use low-salt veggie stock cubes.

sesame spinach and ricotta filo swirl

This classic Greek dish has had a little facelift to make it more family friendly and a touch quicker and easier to assemble. With crisp and flaky pastry on the outside and soft cheesy spinach on the inside, it's moreishly good!

 GF*
 EF*
 V
 Vg*
 DF*

Serves 2 adults and 2 littles

8 cubes of
    frozen spinach
    (approx. 150g/5½oz
    frozen weight)
50g (¼ cup)
    unsalted butter*

250g (1 cup) ricotta
    cheese*
1 tsp garlic paste
50g (1¾oz) Cheddar
    cheese*, finely grated
½ tsp sesame oil

1 egg* (optional)
6 sheets of filo pastry*
1½ tsp sesame seeds
freshly ground
    black pepper

Prep 10 minutes, Bake 25–30 minutes

Freezable

Love your leftovers

Leftovers will keep in the fridge for up to 2–3 days. Enjoy cold or reheat until piping hot in the oven for approx. 5–10 minutes. You can also freeze this dish, but it is best to freeze it before baking, so if you know you want to make this one ahead, possibly making a double batch, freeze the spiral in an airtight container, then place on a baking tray and bake from frozen for 35–45 minutes until piping hot throughout.

Preheat the oven to 200°C fan (220°C/425°F/Gas 7) and set a large non-stick baking tray on the counter ready to use.

Defrost the spinach, either by placing it in the microwave with a splash of water on HIGH for 2½ minutes, or leaving it out at room temperature for a few hours.

Melt the butter in a mug in the microwave for 40–60 seconds or so, ensuring you cover it and keep checking on it, otherwise it'll get too hot and start to bubble and pop in the microwave.

Meanwhile, combine the ricotta, garlic paste, grated Cheddar, sesame oil and some black pepper in a mixing bowl. Add the egg, if using, (this helps firm the mixture up when baked, but it's still delicious without) and mix well.

Add the wilted, defrosted spinach to a fine-mesh sieve over the sink. Use the back of a large spoon to press the mound of spinach down to squeeze out as much water as possible.

Smack the sieve on the work surface to plop the spinach out onto a large chopping board. Briefly run a knife over the spinach to chop it up a little, then add it to the ricotta mixture in the bowl and mix well.

Take the filo pastry and unravel it so you have the multiple sheets of filo stacked on top of each other laid out flat. Liberally spread or brush melted butter across the entire top sheet of pastry, reaching from edge to edge. It's important to work quickly with filo pastry as it dries out very quickly, so there's no need to be neat, just be as quick as you can.

Next, roughly place a third of the ricotta mixture in a sausage-shaped line widthways across the sheet of pastry. Again, there's no need to be neat, just ensure the ricotta mixture pretty much reaches all the way from edge to edge and is fairly even in thickness.

Take the top two sheets of pastry on the pile and roll them up lengthways so you have a long sausage shape with the ricotta filling inside. Transfer this to your baking tray and brush it generously with melted butter. Gently roll it into a spiral shape on the tray – don't worry if you get some tears, you can patch them up with the next piece as you add it to the spiral.

Repeat the process twice more with two lots of two filo sheets, more melted butter and the remaining two thirds of the spinach and ricotta mixture. Add each filo sausage you make onto the end of the spiral on your baking tray, so you're left with one long, continuous spiral shape. Tuck the end of the spiral in slightly so it doesn't catch in the oven and give it all one last brush with butter to ensure there is no dry pastry. Sprinkle the swirl with the sesame seeds, then bake in the preheated oven for 25–30 minutes, until the edges of the pastry have turned golden and crisp.

Serve in slices, with a fresh salad and a little yogurt for dipping, if you like. In general, filo pastry crumbles very well so baby will be able to give it a good go, however, if serving to babies under 1, remove any outer layers of the filo pastry which may be really crisp, just in case they find these bits difficult.

Turn to the next page to see how it looks. I have doubled up on the quantities in the photo to make a bigger swirl for feeding a larger crowd.

Note If you can't get hold of frozen spinach, you can use 300-400g (10½oz–14oz) of fresh spinach. Place it in a large metal sieve and carefully pour over boiling water from the kettle until the spinach is wilted. Press the water out using the back of a spoon, then continue with the recipe.

chicken and butternut squash tray bake

GF*

EF

DF

With notes of lemon and garlic, this simple family meal is easy to prepare and perfect for busy midweek dinners.

Serves 2 adults and 2 littles

Prep 8–10 minutes, Bake 35–45 minutes

Love your leftovers

Leftovers will keep for up to 2 days in the fridge. Reheat the chicken in the oven for around 10–15 minutes until it's piping hot, and pop the couscous in the microwave with a little splash of water for 3–4 minutes on HIGH, stirring halfway through.

6 chicken thighs on the bone, skin on
1 butternut squash, around 1kg/2lb 4oz peeled, deseeded and cut into 1cm (½in) cubes
finely grated zest and juice of

1 unwaxed lemon
2 tsp dried mixed herbs
3 tbsp garlic-infused oil
2 tsp garlic granules
2 heaped tbsp cornflour (cornstarch)
1 tbsp honey (for over 1s) or maple syrup (optional)

1 garlic bulb
160g (1 cup) dried couscous*
1 low-salt chicken stock cube*
freshly ground black pepper

Preheat the oven to 200°C fan (220°C/425°F/Gas 7) and line a very large baking tray with non-stick baking paper or foil.

To a large bowl, add the chicken thighs, butternut squash, lemon zest and juice, dried herbs, 2 tablespoons of the garlic oil, the garlic granules, cornflour and honey or syrup, if using. Add some black pepper and give everything a good stir. Tip the mixture out onto the prepared baking tray.

Arrange the butternut cubes evenly across the tray, then make sure the chicken is nestled between the squash, skin-side up. Drizzle the remaining tablespoon of garlic oil over the chicken skin. Add a sprinkle of S&P to each chicken thigh for adult portions, if you like. Lastly, cut the papery top off the garlic bulb and place it, cut-side down, on the baking tray in one corner. Pop the tray in the preheated oven and bake for 35–45 minutes, until the chicken skin is crispy and the butternut squash is soft and slightly charred.

10 minutes before the bake is done, prep the couscous. Boil the kettle. Add the couscous to a jug, then crumble in the stock cube. Rub the couscous into the stock cube to break up any large pieces. Note the fill line, then pour in water from the kettle to come up to double the amount of couscous. Stir, then cover with a plate and leave until all the water has been absorbed.

Once the chicken and veg are done, transfer the chicken to serving plates. Squeeze out the garlic from inside the bulb, discarding the skin. Use a spoon to mash the garlic into a few bits of squash, then scrape everything from the pan into the bowl of couscous. Stir and serve with the chicken.

For little ones under 3, remove the chicken from the bone and serve in finger strips. For babies under 10 months, remove the chicken skin too and give their squash a little smush with a fork.

gnarly mushroom burgers

I developed this recipe by accident one day when I decided to use up some marinade containing cornflour to coat some large mushrooms. Well, the results were utterly glorious... soft mushroom interior with a crisp, gnarly outside and a smoky flavour from the marinade. I could eat a whole bowl of these.

 GF*

 EF

 V*

 Vg*

 DF

Serves 2 adults and 2 littles

Prep 10 minutes, Bake 28–33 minutes

Freezable

Love your leftovers

Leftovers will keep in the fridge for up to 2 days. Reheat in a hot oven for 10 minutes or until piping hot throughout. You can also freeze the mushrooms and potatoes in an airtight container, then defrost thoroughly before reheating as above.

600g (1lb 5oz) new potatoes, quartered lengthways into wedges
1 tsp garlic granules
2 tsp smoked paprika

1 tsp dried mixed herbs
2 tbsp low-salt soy sauce*
1 tbsp Worcestershire sauce (optional)*
3 tbsp cornflour (cornstarch)

3 tbsp garlic-infused oil
10 large flat mushrooms
4–6 soft burger buns*
freshly ground black pepper

Preheat the oven to 200°C fan (220°C/425°F/Gas 7) and line a very large baking tray with non-stick foil.

Add the quartered new potatoes to a large microwaveable bowl, along with around 100ml (scant ½ cup) of cold tap water. Cover the bowl tightly and microwave on HIGH for 4 minutes.

Meanwhile, make the marinade by combining the garlic granules, smoked paprika, mixed herbs, soy sauce, Worcestershire sauce, if using, and a little black pepper in a bowl. Add 2 tablespoons of the cornflour, 2 tablespoons of the garlic oil and 50ml (scant ¼ cup) of cold tap water and stir well.

Prepare the mushrooms by removing the stalks and brushing off any dirt with a clean tea towel. Don't wash the mushrooms as they will soak up all the water, which would result in a soggy burger.

Once the spuds are done, drain and add them to the bowl of marinade while they're still hot. Stir quickly, then tip them out onto the lined baking tray, ensuring you don't let any excess marinade escape the bowl. Now add the mushrooms to the marinade bowl along with the remaining tablespoon of cornflour. Mix well, but carefully, to avoid breaking the mushrooms, then nestle them between the potatoes on the baking tray, domed-side up (so that the juices don't pool inside them). Ensure everything is evenly spaced out with no overlapping. Drizzle over the remaining 1 tablespoon of garlic oil and pop the tray in the preheated oven for 28–33 minutes until everything is golden and crispy.

These mushrooms and wedges are delicious on their own, but I like to serve them up for burger night. Assemble the burgers with 2–3 mushrooms per bun, depending on the size of your buns. Top with your favourite burger toppings like dips, salad and/or pickles, and serve alongside the new potato wedges. For little ones, serve deconstructed with the mushrooms and burger bun cut into strips.

balsamic chicken tray bake

The balsamic vinegar gives a lovely sweet and sour tang to this dish. Something a little different, but so tasty!

 GF

 EF

 DF

Serves 2 adults and 2 littles

Prep 8–10 minutes, Bake 30–40 minutes

Freezable

Love your leftovers

Leftovers will keep for up to 2 days in the fridge in an airtight container. Or you can freeze leftovers for up to 3 months. Defrost thoroughly in the fridge before reheating in a hot oven for around 10–15 minutes, or until the chicken is piping hot throughout.

4–6 chicken thighs on the bone, skin on
500g (1lb 2oz) large new potatoes, quartered
200g (7oz) cherry tomatoes
½ head of cauliflower, cut into florets

Marinade
4 tbsp balsamic vinegar
1 tbsp honey (for over 1s) or maple syrup (optional)
2 tsp dried mixed herbs
juice of 1 small lemon
1 tsp smoked paprika
3 tsp garlic granules
1 tbsp tomato purée (paste)
3 tbsp garlic-infused oil
a little freshly ground black pepper

Preheat the oven to 200°C fan (220°C/425°F/Gas 7).

Add all the marinade ingredients to a large, high-sided baking tray. Add a splash of water to loosen the consistency and stir well. Add the chicken and gently toss to coat it in the marinade, then move all the chicken pieces to one side of the tray.

Add the potatoes, tomatoes and cauliflower to the tray and stir well to coat in the marinade. Use a spoon to scoop some marinade out from under the chicken and spoon it over the veggies. Now spread the chicken pieces out evenly across the tray, nestled in between the veggies. Try to make sure nothing is overlapping. Shake the pan a little so that everything lays flat, then bake in the preheated oven for 30–40 minutes until the chicken and potatoes have cooked through and turned crispy on top. Keep an eye on it from the 30-minute mark to ensure nothing is burning in the oven.

Serve as is, with the chicken removed from the bone in finger strips for little ones under 3, and with the chicken skin removed too for little ones under 10 months. Adults, add a little more salt and pepper to your portion, if you wish.

lamb and tomato hot pot

With succulent lamb and tender veg in a rich tomato sauce topped with crispy scalloped potatoes, this is a real one-pot wonder! The minimal washing up is such a bonus.

Serves 2 adults and 3 kids

Prep 10 minutes, Bake 1 hour

Freezable

Love your leftovers

Leftovers will keep for up to 2 days in the fridge. Reheat in a hot oven for approx. 15–20 minutes or in a microwave on HIGH for a few minutes or until piping hot. You can also freeze cooled leftovers in an airtight container, defrosting them thoroughly before reheating as above.

500g (1lb 2oz) lean minced (ground) lamb
1 brown onion
3 large carrots
2 low-salt beef or chicken stock cubes*

1 tbsp Worcestershire sauce*
2 tbsp tomato purée (paste)
2 tsp garlic paste
2 tbsp cornflour (cornstarch)

500g (1lb 2oz) passata (strained tomatoes)
2 tsp dried mixed herbs
3–4 large all-rounder potatoes, washed
2 tsp garlic-infused oil, plus extra if needed

Preheat the oven to 180°C fan (200°C/400°F/Gas 6) and put the kettle on to boil.

Place a large casserole pot on the hob over a high heat to heat up. Add the lamb mince and let it cook for 1 minute without touching while you dice the onion. Now, break up the mince using a wooden spoon and add the onion, stirring it in. If your mince is very lean and looks like it is sticking, then add a drizzle of garlic oil.

Let the meat cook while you peel the carrots and cut them into chunks. Turn your attention back to the pot and crumble in the stock cubes, add the Worcestershire sauce, tomato purée, garlic paste and cornflour. Cook, stirring, for 1 minute, then add the chopped carrots, passata and mixed herbs. Stir well, then top the pot up with boiling water out of the kettle to reach about 1–2cm (½–¾in) over everything. The amount of water you need really depends on the size of your pot, so play it by ear. Try not to add too much water, though, as the potatoes on top will sink down below the sauce once baked, which is not a bad thing taste-wise, but it won't look as pretty.

Stir well and allow it to bubble while you slice the potatoes into 0.5cm (¼in) thick rounds – don't worry about peeling them to save time. Scrape the bottom of the pot with your wooden spoon to loosen any stuck-on bits, then take the pot off the heat to add the potatoes. Layer the sliced potatoes over the top of the pot carefully, as the sauce will be hot. Try to overlap them a little to give a pretty design, then drizzle over a little garlic oil to help the potatoes crisp up. If you're using a narrow, deep pot, your potatoes may sink into the sauce, so in this case just add an extra layer or two of sliced potatoes on top.

Pop the dish in the preheated oven, uncovered, for 1 hour to bake. Allow to stand for 5 minutes before serving, and take care as it will be really hot! If there's a little bit of lamb fat sitting on the top of the potatoes or around the edge of the pot, use a spoon to gently skim this away before serving.

Serve as is, with a little veg on the side – Savoy cabbage works perfectly.

broccoli toad-in-the-hole

A veggie take on the British classic. Nutritious broccoli is coated in a luscious, thick, cheesy Yorkshire pudding batter. This is fab as a finger food on a picky lunch plate, or serve with gravy or even as a side to your Sunday roast.

 GF*

 V

 DF*

Makes 9 squares

Prep 10 minutes, Bake 25–30 minutes

Freezable

Love your leftovers

Leftovers will keep for up to 3 days in the fridge or freeze for up to 3 months. To reheat from fresh, place back in a hot oven for 10–15 minutes until piping hot throughout. It may need a splash of water to add a touch more moisture, or a little drizzle of oil on top before reheating. To reheat from frozen, add an extra 5–10 minutes of baking time.

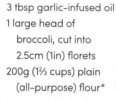

3 tbsp garlic-infused oil
1 large head of broccoli, cut into 2.5cm (1in) florets
200g (1⅔ cups) plain (all-purpose) flour*
100g (3½oz) Cheddar cheese*, grated
1 tsp dried mixed herbs
1 tsp garlic granules
4 large eggs
220ml (1 cup) milk*
freshly ground black pepper

Preheat the oven to 220°C fan (240°C/475°F/Gas 9).

Add the garlic oil to a 20cm (8in) square brownie tin, or something of a similar size. Add the broccoli florets to the tin and stir to coat the broccoli in the oil. Pop it in the preheated oven for 7–8 minutes, or until the veg is starting to just turn brown on the edges. It should smell lovely and nutty.

While the broccoli roasts, make the batter. In a mixing bowl, stir together the flour, grated cheese, dried herbs, garlic granules, eggs and a good grinding of black pepper. Slowly add the milk and mix to form a smooth batter.

Once the broccoli is done, remove the tin from the oven and quickly close the oven door to avoid lots of heat escaping. You want to work quickly here to make sure both the pan and the oil stay as hot as possible. Roughly stir the broccoli, then pour the batter into the pan. Push any pieces of broccoli that stick up down into the batter so they're completely submerged. Get the pan back into the oven on the top shelf where the oven is at its hottest.

Bake for 25–30 minutes, or until the top is deliciously golden. Be mindful to avoid opening the oven door for the first 20 minutes, as this will let hot air escape which is needed to help the batter rise.

Serve in squares or finger strips as a main meal or a side dish.

lemon bread chicken bake

There is something utterly comforting about this simple dish. The chicken juices seep down into the bread and broccoli below, making them flavourful and full of umami deliciousness. Whilst the veg cooks, steam rises and ensures the chicken on top stays beautifully succulent, with the best crispy skin! My daughter Nina said this one was her favourite.

Serves 2 adults and 2 littles

Prep 7–8 minutes, Cook 40–55 minutes

Freezable

Love your leftovers

Leftovers will keep for up to 3 days in the fridge, and they make the best sarnie!! OR, you can pop the dish back into a hot oven for 10–15 minutes or until the chicken is piping hot throughout. Alternatively, freeze for up to 3 months. Defrost thoroughly before reheating as above.

4–5 thick slices of slightly stale bread*
1 head of broccoli, cut into medium florets
1½ tbsp garlic-infused oil
juice of 1 lemon
1 tsp garlic granules
1 tsp dried mixed herbs
approx. 60g (2oz) Cheddar cheese*
5–6 chicken thighs on the bone, skin on
freshly ground black pepper

Preheat the oven to 200°C fan (220°C/425°F/Gas 7) and find an oven dish with high sides that will fit the chicken snugly inside.

Tear or cut the bread into chunks, approx. 2.5 cm (1in) wide and add them to the oven dish, along with the broccoli florets. Add 1 tablespoon of the garlic oil, the lemon juice, garlic granules, dried herbs and a good grinding of black pepper. Grate the cheese over the whole lot, then using two big spoons, mix well to ensure every piece of bread has some flavour stuck to it.

Make sure the broccoli in the dish is distributed evenly, then use the back of a spoon to press everything down so no broccoli or bread is sticking up too much, so that they don't burn in the oven.

Place the chicken thighs on top of the bread and broccoli, skin-side up. Ensure the chicken pieces aren't overlapping and that the skin is not bunched up anywhere. Ideally, you want any excess skin hanging out towards the edge of the dish, rather than in the middle, to help it get crispy. Drizzle over the remaining garlic oil and add more black pepper. You can also salt the chicken skin if you like, and just remove it if serving to little ones.

Pop the whole dish, uncovered, on the middle shelf of the preheated oven to bake for around 40–45 minutes, or until the chicken skin has turned crisp and the chicken is cooked throughout.

Remove the dish from the oven and preheat the grill to high.

Remove the chicken pieces from the dish and place them on a plate to rest. Give the bread and broccoli a stir, then place under the hot grill for 3–5 minutes to help it char and turn a little crispier on the edges.

Serve the bake on plates with a little salad, if you wish. If serving to little ones under 3, remove the chicken from the bone and cut into finger strips.

Note You can swap the bread for 400–500g (14oz–1lb 2oz) of diced new potatoes. They will soak up all the delicious chicken juices as they cook too.

family-friendly bean enchiladas

This is a simple bean enchilada recipe, but feel free to add roasted veggies or chopped pre-cooked meat like chicken to the filling before rolling.

 GF*

 EF

 V*

 Vg*

 DF*

Serves 2 adults and 2–4 littles

Prep 10–12 minutes, Bake 20–30 minutes

Freezable

Love your leftovers

Leftovers will keep for up to 3 days in the fridge. To reheat, transfer the enchiladas to a smaller dish, add a sprinkling of water and reheat in a hot oven for 10 minutes or until piping hot inside. You can also freeze leftovers; allow to cool, then carefully lift each enchilada onto a sheet of foil. Wrap it up tightly, then reheat in an oven dish in a hot oven for 15 minutes. Remove the foil and bake for a further 5–10 minutes until piping hot.

2 tsp cooking oil, for greasing
400g (14oz) passata (strained tomatoes)
1 low-salt chicken or vegetable stock cube*, crumbled
2 tsp tomato purée (paste)

1 tbsp cornflour (cornstarch)
1 tsp sugar (optional)
2 x 400g (14oz) cans of mixed beans in unsalted water, drained
3 tsp smoked paprika
1 tsp ground cumin

100g (3½oz) Cheddar cheese*, grated
2 tsp garlic granules
1 tsp dried mixed herbs
250g (9oz) packet of ready-cooked rice
6 large tortilla wraps*
freshly ground black pepper

Preheat the oven to 200°C fan (220°C/425°F/Gas 7) and grease a large ceramic oven dish with the oil. Fill the kettle and put it on to boil.

Combine roughly 150g (5½oz) of the passata with the crumbled stock cube, tomato purée, cornflour and sugar, if using, in a large, heatproof bowl. Stir very well, then pour in 250ml (generous 1 cup) of boiling water from the kettle. Stir well again, it will thicken just a touch.

Add the drained canned beans to a large, flat-bottomed bowl, then use a potato masher to mash and break down the beans until there are no whole beans left. Add half of the tomato sauce you've just made, along with the rest of the passata, the paprika, cumin, half of the grated cheese, the garlic granules and dried herbs. Squeeze the rice packet to break up the grains, then add this to the bowl and give it all a really good stir.

Now it's time to roll. Lay a tortilla wrap out on a clean work surface and add 3 heaped tablespoons of the bean mixture to the centre. Tuck in each side before rolling up, then transfer the filled wrap to the oven dish, seam-side down. I like to roll up the kid's portions, then add salt to the remaining bean mixture, or even chilli sauce, before rolling up the rest. Alternatively, season yours once it's cooked so you don't forget whose is whose!

Repeat the wrapping process for the remaining tortillas and bean filling until they're all in the oven dish. Quickly pour over any remaining beany tomato sauce, then sprinkle over the remaining grated cheese.

Pop the dish in the preheated oven to bake for 20–30 minutes, or until the cheese has melted and turned golden.

Serve with sour cream and avocado, ideally, or a simple side salad is delicious too.

creamy sweet potato, mushroom and chicken tray bake

Here's my one-pan, oven-roasted version of a stroganoff. As this dish bakes, the chicken juices soak into the sweet potato, making it lusciously tender, ready to be mashed and turned into a delightful creamy sauce.

 GF*

 EF

 DF*

Serves 2 adults and 3 hungry children

Prep 10 minutes, Bake 35 minutes

Freezable

Love your leftovers

Leftovers will keep for up to 2–3 days in the fridge. To reheat, bake the chicken in the oven for 10 minutes until piping hot throughout. Warm the sauce up in a saucepan over a gentle heat on the hob until piping hot. You can also reheat the entire dish in the microwave for 2–3 minutes. This dish will freeze for up to 2 months, defrost it thoroughly and then reheat as above.

650g (1lb 7oz) sweet potatoes
1 low-salt chicken stock cube*
200g (7oz) chestnut or button mushrooms
10g (¼oz) dried porcini mushrooms

2 tsp garlic granules
2 tsp dried mixed herbs
1kg (2lb 4oz) chicken drumsticks, thighs or leg pieces, skin on
2 tbsp garlic-infused oil
1 whole garlic bulb

200ml (scant 1 cup) crème fraîche*
freshly ground black pepper
2 tbsp finely chopped fresh chives, to garnish

Preheat the oven to 200°C fan (220°C/425°F/Gas 7). Find a very large baking tray with slightly high sides – it needs to be at least 25 x 35cm (10 x 14in) in size. Fill the kettle with water and put it on to boil.

Peel the sweet potatoes and cut them into cubes of around 2cm (¾in). Add the sweet potato cubes to a microwaveable bowl along with a dash of water. Cover and cook on HIGH for 3 minutes.

Meanwhile, pour 450ml (1¾ cups) of boiling water from the kettle into a jug, crumble in the stock cube and stir to dissolve. Add the stock to the baking tray, along with the fresh mushrooms, dried mushrooms, garlic granules and 1 teaspoon of the dried mixed herbs. Stir well, then drain any water from the sweet potatoes, add them to the tray and stir.

Lay the chicken on top of everything, skin-side up. Drizzle the garlic oil over all the ingredients in the tray, paying most attention to the chicken skin. Add the remaining mixed herbs and a little black pepper to the chicken. Cut off the top of the garlic bulb, revealing the cloves inside, then nestle the bulb between the chicken pieces, cut-side down. Bake in the preheated oven for 35 minutes until the chicken is cooked through and the skin is golden.

Remove the chicken pieces from the tray and place them on a separate plate to rest. Using a piece of kitchen paper or a tea towel so that you don't burn your hands, squeeze the soft roasted garlic out of the bulb back into the baking tray, discarding the skin. Add the crème fraîche to the baking tray. Using a potato masher, mash and stir all the sauce components in the tray together so that the sweet potatoes break down and combine with the liquid. Place the chicken back in the tray and sprinkle everything with the chopped chives before serving. For little ones, remove the chicken from the bone, or allow them to hold and eat the drumstick independently. Do be vigilant to ensure little one doesn't struggle with the cartilage joint or come into contact with the sharp bone that sits inside the drumstick.

speedy beef and dumpling stew

Normally this comfort food favourite takes a long time to make, bubbling away on the stovetop or in the slow cooker for hours. Well, if you have the craving but not much time until dinner, then give this one a go. It's ready in about 30 minutes.

Serves 2 adults and 2 littles

Prep 10 minutes, Cook 20–30 minutes

Freezable

Love your leftovers

Leftovers will keep for up to 2–3 days in the fridge. Reheat in a saucepan until bubbling and piping hot throughout. You can also freeze leftovers for up to 3 months, defrosting them thoroughly before reheating as above.

- 500g (1lb 2oz) lean minced (ground) beef
- 3 large carrots, washed
- 200g (7oz) chestnut or button mushrooms
- 2 tbsp tomato purée (paste)
- 220g (1⅔ cups) self-raising flour*
- 100g (scant 1 cup) shredded beef or vegetarian suet*
- 2 low-salt beef stock cubes*
- 1 heaped tbsp cornflour (cornstarch)
- 2 tsp garlic paste
- 2 tsp dried mixed herbs
- 2 tbsp Worcestershire sauce*
- a generous amount of freshly ground black pepper

Set a large saucepan over a high heat to warm up. Fill the kettle and put it on to boil.

Add the minced beef to the hot pan and break it up into pieces with a wooden spoon. Let the meat cook while you grate the carrots and mushrooms on a box grater. Add the grated veg to the beef along with the tomato purée. Stir well, then leave to cook for 3 more minutes.

Meanwhile, make the dumplings. Add the flour and suet to a mixing bowl, then pour in 240ml (1 cup) of cold water. Stir until the mixture forms a batter, then set aside.

Back to the saucepan, crumble in the stock cubes, then add the cornflour and stir for 30 seconds. Pour in around 1.2 litres/2 pints of boiling water out of the kettle – or enough to cover the mince plus 2.5cm (1in) or so. Add the garlic paste, mixed herbs, Worcestershire sauce and black pepper, stir well and bring to the boil.

Use two tablespoons to dollop heaped spoonfuls of the dumpling batter into the pan, spacing them apart so that they don't overlap. The mixture will be very soft and sticky so it's easier to use spoons to do this, rather than rolling the mixture into balls.

Pop the lid on the pan, turn the heat down slightly to medium-high and cook for 20–30 minutes; don't remove the lid for at least 20 minutes or your dumplings may sink. You'll know it's ready when the dumplings have pretty much doubled in size and look fluffier.

Serve in big bowls and cut the dumplings into thick strips for baby, if you like. Adults, you may like a little salt and more pepper on your portion for extra seasoning.

oat-crumbed roasted fruit

Think of this dish as an easier crumble – just throw it all in the pan and let it do its thing!
The soft roasted plums and nectarines are bursting with natural sweetness and the oats
give a lovely crunch.

 GF*

 EF

 V

 Vg*

 DF*

**Serves 2 adults
and 2 littles**

4 ripe nectarines, cut
into wedges and
stones removed

4 ripe plums, cut into
wedges and stones
removed

1½ tbsp cornflour
(cornstarch)

2 tsp ground cinnamon

1½ tbsp light soft brown
sugar (optional)

7 heaped tbsp rolled
porridge oats*

3½ tbsp chilled unsalted
butter*, cubed

**Prep 7 minutes,
Bake 20–25
minutes**

Preheat the oven to 180°C fan (200°C/400°F/Gas 6).

Add the fruit to a large, shallow-sided baking tray. Sprinkle over the
cornflour, cinnamon, sugar, if using, and oats. Give it all a good stir to coat
the fruit with all the ingredients. Shake the tray so the fruit separates and is
evenly spaced apart – ideally there should be a bit of space between the
fruit wedges and they shouldn't be bunched up.

Dot the cubed butter over the top, then pop the tray in the preheated oven.

Freezable

After 15 minutes, using a fish slice, lift and scrape the fruit from the bottom
of the tray, flipping over any large clumps. Pop the tray back in the oven
and bake for a further 5–10 minutes until the fruit is super soft and the oats
have taken on a nutty smell and golden colour. Be sure to regularly check
they're not burning as the sugars in the fruit can catch easily.

**Love your
leftovers**

Leftovers will keep
for up to 2–3 days in
the fridge, they can
be enjoyed cold or
you can reheat
them in a hot oven
until piping hot –
they're delicious
on porridge for
breakfast too! This
dish can be frozen
for up to 3 months.
Defrost thoroughly
before enjoying
cold or reheating
in the oven
as above.

Remove from the oven and allow to stand for 5–10 minutes to firm up a
little and cool, as the fruit will be super hot. Serve with yogurt, custard or
my Cherry and Mango Frozen Yogurt (see page 229).

cherry bakewell flapjacks

Soft oats, deliciously flavoured with almond and bursting with the jammy flavours of sweet, juicy cherries that bejewel the top. These are perfect for breakfast, as an afternoon snack and even for pudding – a tasty low-sugar treat!

 GF*
 EF
 V
 Vg*
 DF*

Makes 16 flapjacks

Prep 10 minutes, Bake 17–22 minutes

Freezable

Love your leftovers

Store in an airtight container for up to 3 days at room temperature, or keep in the freezer for up to 3 months. Either defrost at room temperature and enjoy within 24 hours, or defrost and reheat in a hot oven until piping hot throughout. Delicious served with ice cream!

1 x 410g (14oz) can of prunes in fruit juice
2 tsp almond extract
100g (1 cup) ground almonds

350g (3½ cups) rolled porridge oats*
150g (⅔ cup) unsalted butter, melted *

200g (1¼ cups) frozen dark sweet pitted cherries (unsweetened)

Preheat the oven to 180°C fan (200°C/400°F/Gas 6) and line a 20cm (8in) square brownie tin with non-stick baking paper.

Add the prunes, along with the juice, to a mixing bowl. If they haven't already been pitted, take each prune and squish it in your hand to find and remove the stone. Then take a potato masher or the back of a large ladle and squash the fruit to turn it into a purée – this will also help you find any stones you may have missed.

Next, add the almond extract and ground almonds to the prune purée and stir well. Add the oats and melted butter before giving one final stir, ensuring that all the oats are coated and starting to soak up the liquid.

Pour the mixture into your prepared tin and spread it out evenly. Using the back of a tablespoon, even out the top of the flapjack, making sure there are no lumps and bumps.

Scatter the frozen cherries over the top (no need to defrost) and, using your palm, press the fruit into the flapjack to embed it into the oats.

Bake in the centre of your preheated oven for 17–22 minutes until the edges of the oats are turning golden and the cherries have burst their juices into the flapjack.

Remove from the oven and allow the flapjack to cool in the tin for 5 minutes before using the baking paper to lift the entire bake out of the tin and onto a chopping board. Cut into 16 squares and enjoy warm or cold with a little yogurt, if you like.

slow cooker

Prep in 10 minutes or less, throw all the ingredients into your slow cooker pot and allow the dish to simmer away for hours whilst you get on with your day. I love that your house always smells so good as you wait for dinnertime – I find it makes the meal taste even better, don't you?

hidden veg tomato soup

This vibrant soup is bursting with flavour and packed with veggies. The kids will willingly gobble it all up!

 GF*

 EF

 V*

 Vg*

 DF

Serves 3 adults and 2 littles

Prep 10 minutes, Cook 3–9 hours

Freezable

Love your leftovers

Leftovers will keep for up to 2–3 days in the fridge, or freeze for up to 4 months. Add to a saucepan to melt and reheat until bubbling.

1 red or yellow pepper, deseeded and roughly chopped
4 celery sticks, roughly chopped
2 leeks, slit open and washed, roughly chopped
3 garlic cloves, peeled
1 low-salt chicken or vegetable stock cube*
2 tsp dried mixed herbs
2 heaped tsp smoked paprika
1 tbsp light soft brown sugar (optional)
1 x 260g (11oz) can of unsalted sweetcorn in water
3 x 400g (14oz) cans of peeled plum tomatoes in tomato juice
freshly ground black pepper
fresh basil leaves, to garnish (optional)

Add the roughly chopped pepper, celery and leeks to the slow cooker along with the peeled garlic. Crumble in the stock cube, add the dried herbs, smoked paprika and sugar, if using. Add the entire can of sweetcorn, including the water, and a good grinding of black pepper.

Empty the cans of tomatoes into the slow cooker, then fill them each with a small amount of tap water – no more than a quarter of the can – and swill out any remaining tomato, pouring the liquid into the slow cooker pot too. Stir very well and pop the lid on to cook for a minimum of 3 hours on HIGH or up to 8–9 hours on LOW. This recipe is a good one if you will be out all day and want to come home to a dinner that's ready.

Once the veggies are soft, simply blend using a stick blender until smooth. The soup is now ready to serve in bowls topped with black pepper and fresh basil leaves to garnish, if you wish. Adults may like a tiny pinch of extra sugar and a little salt for added seasoning.

If you have time, I prefer to add an extra step and sieve this soup to remove any pulp – the kiddos may prefer it this way too (the soup has not been sieved for this recipe photo). Add a touch of boiling water if you'd prefer to thin down the soup to perfect bread dunking consistency, or keep it thick to serve with pasta.

If you would like to adapt this dish into a delicious hidden veggie pasta sauce, skip the step of adding water to the tomato cans and drain the sweetcorn can before adding it to the slow cooker. This way the finished sauce will be much thicker and better for coating your pasta – perfect with a little grated cheese, too.

No slow cooker? Add all of the ingredients to a large lidded saucepan. Bring to the boil over a high heat, then reduce the heat to low and simmer for about 30–40 minutes until the veg is tender. Blitz and finish as above.

slow-cooked pulled chicken tikka

The throw it-all-in kinda dish that we crave on busy days! Serve over rice or with potatoes, or how about even using the pulled chicken as a filling for a different take on lasagne? Any leftovers are also delicious in a warmed wrap or toasted panini.

 GF

 EF

 V*

 DF*

Serves 2 adults and 2 littles

Prep 5 minutes, Slow cook 4 hours

Freezable

Love your leftovers

Leftovers will keep for up to 3 days in the fridge. To reheat, pop in the microwave on HIGH for 2–3 minutes, or heat in a lidded saucepan for 5–10 minutes until piping hot throughout. You can also freeze this for up to 2 months. Defrost and reheat in the microwave for 3-4 minutes on HIGH, or defrost in the fridge, then reheat as above.

1 onion
1 tsp very mild chilli powder (or as hot as your family like it)
1 tsp ground turmeric
1 tsp ground coriander
1 tsp ground cumin
2 tbsp smoked paprika
2 tbsp sweet paprika

2 tsp mild garam masala
3 garlic cloves, crushed
2 tbsp garlic-infused oil
2 tbsp tomato purée (paste)
6 skinless boneless chicken thighs or 4 chicken breasts*

2–3 heaped tbsp thick Greek yogurt or double (heavy) cream* (optional)
freshly ground black pepper

Chop the top off the onion, but leave the root attached. Peel off the skin and pull it over the root where it is still connected. Use the attached onion skin as your handle to hold the onion while you grate the flesh using the coarse side of a box grater.

Add the grated onion pulp and any juice to the slow cooker, along with all the spices, the garlic, garlic oil, tomato purée and a generous grinding of black pepper. Mix well, then add the chicken before mixing again.

Put the lid on and cook on LOW for 3–4 hours, or until the chicken is very tender and shreds easily. Using a wooden spoon, mix the chicken firmly into the sauce to shred it up – it should be so soft that it easily falls apart.

This is delicious to eat as it is now, but you can also add Greek yogurt or a splash of double cream to turn this into a creamy curry.

No slow cooker? Add all the ingredients to a lidded ovenproof casserole dish. Bake in an oven preheated to 160°C fan (180°C/350°F/Gas 4) with the lid on for 2-2½ hours. You can also use a high-sided oven dish and cover it with foil if you don't have a lidded dish.

Veggie swaps
Swap the chicken for butternut squash or aubergine (eggplant) cubes for a veg-filled curry instead. For extra protein, try adding some cooked canned lentils too.

Family fish
The fish fillets will shrink
a little when cooked,
so for a hungry family
of 4 I recommend
cooking 6 fillets.

tomato and spinach fish stew

When I think of slow cooker meals, fish doesn't usually come to mind. However, this dish gives you soft and flaky delicate fish in a rich, flavourful tomato and spinach sauce. As a bonus, this recipe calls for frozen fish cooked straight from the freezer, which is such an easy and economical way of adding fish to our diet.

 GF*

 EF

 DF

Serves 2 adults and 2 littles

Prep 5 minutes, Cook 3–7 hours

Freezable

Love your leftovers

This dish is best served fresh, however, if you have any leftovers, these will keep for up to 24 hours in the fridge. To reheat, place in an ovenproof dish, cover with foil and heat in a hot oven for 10–15 minutes until piping hot throughout. You can also freeze any leftovers for up to 1 month. Defrost in the fridge and then reheat as above.

500g (1lb 2oz) crushed tomatoes or passata (strained tomatoes)
8 cubes of chopped frozen spinach
1 x 400g (14oz) can of coconut milk
2 tsp sweet paprika
2 tsp smoked paprika
1 tsp dried mixed herbs
2 tsp garlic granules OR 2 garlic cloves, minced
2 tbsp tomato purée (paste)
1 tsp sugar (optional)
1 low-salt chicken or vegetable stock cube*, crumbled
4–6 frozen skinless and boneless large white fish fillets, e.g. haddock, bass, pollock or cod

Add the crushed tomatoes or passata to the slow cooker pot along with the frozen spinach, coconut milk, sweet and smoked paprika, dried herbs, garlic granules or fresh garlic, tomato purée, sugar, if using, and crumbled stock cube. Give it all a really good stir so that there are no lumps apart from the frozen spinach, which will defrost as it cooks. Pop the lid on and cook on HIGH for 3 hours or on LOW for 5–6 hours.

The smell in your kitchen will be divine when the cooking time is up. Give the sauce another good stir so that any small lumps of stock cube that have melted during cooking are distributed evenly through the sauce.

Now, take the fish out of the freezer and add the frozen fillets to the sauce. Stir and make sure each fillet is submerged in the sauce, then put the lid back on and cook for a further 30–40 minutes on HIGH or 50–60 minutes on LOW, or until the fish flakes easily, as this will tell you that it's done. To double check, lift up one fish fillet gently using a fish slice, then gently flake it in half at its thickest point. Place your finger on the white fish flesh inside, if it's too hot to keep your finger there for a few seconds, then it's done. If it feels just lukewarm, you need to cook it for another 10–20 minutes until piping hot.

Serve alongside some rice to soak up the sauce or crusty bread for dipping.

No slow cooker? Cook the tomato sauce in a large, high-sided frying pan with a lid on for at least 30 minutes over a medium heat on the hob – the longer the better really. When the sauce is done, add the fish and cook for a further 15 minutes or until the fish is piping hot throughout.

chinese mushroom curry

Mushrooms are slow-cooked until silky soft in this mild Chinese-style curry sauce, making for a simple yet delicious meal. Feel free to replace the chestnut mushrooms with 6 diced chicken thighs or a cubed butternut squash for a little more variety.

Serves 3 adults and 2 littles

Prep 8 minutes, Slow cook 2–4 hours

Freezable

Love your leftovers

Leftovers will keep in the fridge for up to 3 days. Reheat in a saucepan until piping hot and bubbling. This dish will also freeze for up to 3 months. Defrost at room temperature and reheat as above, or defrost and reheat in the microwave for 3–4 minutes until piping hot throughout.

250g (9oz) button mushrooms
1 brown onion
2 heaped tbsp cornflour (cornstarch)
2 large garlic cloves, minced or crushed
1½ tsp ground turmeric

1 low-salt chicken or vegetable stock cube*, crumbled
2 tsp mild curry powder
2 tbsp low-salt soy sauce*
2 large handfuls of frozen peas

500g (1lb 2oz) chestnut mushrooms (or extra button mushrooms)
1 x 400g (14oz) can of coconut milk
a little freshly ground black pepper

Grate the button mushrooms and the onion on a box grater, or pulse them in a food processor until finely chopped.

Add the onion and mushroom pulp and any escaping juices to the slow cooker. Add the cornflour, garlic, turmeric, crumbled stock cube, curry powder, soy sauce, frozen peas and a little black pepper.

Either quarter the chestnut mushrooms or cut them into chunky strips (which may be easier for little ones under 2 to hold and eat), then add these to the slow cooker too. Give everything a good stir to dissolve the cornflour. Stir in the coconut milk, then quarter-fill the empty can with cold tap water to swill out any remaining coconut milk, adding this to the pot too.

Place the lid on the slow cooker and cook on HIGH for 2 hours or on LOW for 3–4 hours. Serve with naan bread or over rice to soak up all the delicious sauce. Adults may want an extra dash of soy sauce or a sprinkling of salt.

Note If you're serving to under 1s, they may struggle with the chunks of mushroom, so grate a higher proportion of your mushrooms, or alternatively blend up their sauce a little.

No slow cooker? Sauté the onion and chopped button mushrooms in a large saucepan with a touch of oil on the hob for a few minutes until the onion is translucent, then add the remaining ingredients. Simmer for 20–30 minutes or until the sauce has thickened and the mushrooms have cooked.

smoky pork and bean stew

Make your home smell amazing all day with this warming slow-cooked recipe. The aroma invites you to dig right into this bowl of comforting goodness.

Serves 2 adults and 3 littles

Prep 10 minutes, Cook 4–7 hours

Freezable

Love your leftovers

Leftovers can be kept for up to 3 days in the fridge or frozen for up to 3 months. Reheat in a saucepan until bubbling and piping hot throughout. Defrost thoroughly before reheating in the same way if you have frozen the stew.

1 tbsp garlic-infused oil
approx. 500g (1lb 2oz)
pork loin or belly, cut
into 2.5cm (1in)
chunks
2 tbsp plain
(all-purpose) flour*
3 x 400g (14oz) cans of
mixed beans in water

1 low-salt chicken stock
cube*
1 tbsp Worcestershire
sauce*
1 tbsp tomato purée
(paste)
1 tsp dried mixed herbs
2 tsp garlic granules OR
2 garlic cloves,
crushed

2 tbsp smoked paprika
400g (14oz) carrots,
peeled and cut into
large chunks
freshly ground black
pepper

Get a large, non-stick frying pan over a medium-high heat and add the garlic oil. Put the kettle on to boil.

Meanwhile, toss the meat in the plain flour, then add to the hot frying pan. Sear the meat on all sides, trying not to touch it too much as this will slow down the caramelization which brings out all the flavour.

Add the cans of beans (including the water) to the slow-cooker pot. Crumble the stock cube into one of the empty bean cans, then carefully quarter-fill the can with boiling water out of the kettle. Stir to dissolve the stock cube, then add the liquid to the slow cooker along with the Worcestershire sauce, tomato purée, dried herbs, garlic granules or fresh garlic, smoked paprika, carrots and a generous grinding of black pepper.

Once the meat has turned golden on all sides, add this too and give everything a good stir. Cook on HIGH for 4 hours or on LOW for 6–7 hours, or until the meat is falling apart and the stew is thick and oozy.

Serve in big bowls, with a chunk of bread for dipping.

A note on beans You can use any canned beans you fancy for this recipe (cannellini, pinto, borlotti, black beans, kidney beans, etc.) Just ensure they are in water and not brine, and there is no added salt. You can also mix and match beans – you can't go wrong here.

No slow cooker? Sear the meat in the oil in a large lidded pot or ovenproof dish. Add the remaining ingredients, cover and cook on the hob over a low heat for at least 2 hours until the meat is tender. Or, cook in an oven preheated to 160°C fan (180°C/350°F/Gas 4) for a similar time.

Choosing your pork
When buying the pork, try to find a good ratio of meat to fat. You want a little fat as this gives lots of flavour and juiciness, however, if there's too much fat, this will all melt away during cooking and your stew will be left a little meatless.

slow cooker lamb tagine

With tender lamb, rich sauce and Moroccan flavours of cumin, cinnamon and chickpeas, this throw-it-all-in recipe is the perfect comfort food on a cold, wintery day.

Serves 2 adults and 3 littles

Prep 10 minutes, Cook 4–7 hours

Freezable

Love your leftovers

Leftovers will keep for up to 2 days in the fridge. Reheat in a saucepan until bubbling and piping hot throughout. Or, you can freeze the tagine for up to 2 months and defrost thoroughly before reheating as above.

1–2 tbsp sunflower oil
750g (1lb 10oz) lamb shoulder, diced and most of the excess fat removed
1 large brown onion
3 large carrots
2 tsp ground cumin
2 tsp sweet paprika

1 x 400g (14oz) can of chickpeas in water, drained
1 x 400g (14oz) can of chopped (diced) tomatoes
2 low-salt chicken or beef stock cubes*, crumbled

2 large garlic cloves, crushed
½ tsp ground cinnamon
a handful of seedless raisins (optional)
fresh herbs, to garnish (optional)

Set a large frying pan over a high heat and add 1 tablespoon of sunflower oil. Fill the kettle and put it on to boil.

Once the oil is hot, add half of the lamb to the pan, spread it out in an even layer and leave to fry for 2 minutes until the outside of the meat is nicely browned. Use a spatula to turn the meat over and leave to fry for a further 1–2 minutes. Transfer the browned meat to the slow cooker and repeat the browning process with the remaining lamb and another tablespoon of oil.

Meanwhile, grate or finely dice the onion, peel the carrots and cut them into chunks. Add these to the slow cooker, along with the rest of the ingredients.

When all the meat is browned and in the slow cooker, add 400ml (1⅔ cups) of boiling water from the kettle to the empty hot frying pan. Stir with a wooden spoon for 30 seconds to let the water soak up any caramelized bits of meat from the base of the pan, as this is where the flavour is. Pour this flavoured water into the slow cooker.

Give it all a really good stir and pop the lid on. Cook on HIGH for 4 hours or on LOW for 6–7 hours until the meat is super tender.

Serve in big bowls with boiled potatoes to soak up all the juices and fresh herbs to garnish, if you like. Chickpeas are usually too small to be a hazard for little taste testers, however, feel free to mash them with a fork before serving, if you prefer.

No slow cooker? Brown the meat in the oil in a casserole pot before adding all of the remaining ingredients. Cover and cook over a low heat on the hob for 2 hours or in an oven preheated to 160°C fan (180°C/350°F/Gas 4) for 2–3 hours.

slow cooker broccoli beef

Succulent beef and nutritious broccoli in a flavourful Chinese-style sauce. This is so quick to whip up at lunchtime, you'll feel smug all afternoon knowing dinner will be a doddle!

Serves 2 adults and 2 littles

Prep 7 minutes, Cook 2–4 hours

Freezable

Love your leftovers

Leftovers (without rice or noodles) will keep for up to 2 days in the fridge. Reheat in the microwave for 2–3 minutes on HIGH or in a saucepan until piping hot throughout. Once cooled completely, you can also freeze the broccoli beef for up to 2 months. Defrost thoroughly and reheat as above.

2 low-salt beef or vegetable stock cubes*
600g (1lb 5oz) stewing steak (beef)
1½ tsp sesame oil
3 tbsp low-salt soy sauce*
4 garlic cloves, minced
2 tbsp sesame seeds, plus 1 tbsp extra to serve
2 tsp sugar (optional)
2 heaped tbsp cornflour (cornstarch)
1 large head of broccoli, cut into large florets
thinly sliced spring onion (scallion), to garnish (optional)

Boil the kettle, then add 700ml (scant 3 cups) of boiling water to a measuring jug. Crumble in the stock cubes and stir to dissolve them.

Cut the steak into 1.5cm (⅝in) wide strips. Add the meat to the slow cooker along with the hot beef stock, sesame oil, soy sauce, garlic, sesame seeds and sugar, if using. Stir the ingredients together well and put the lid on. Cook for 4 hours on LOW or for 2–3 hours on HIGH.

Once the beef is tender, make a cornflour slurry by mixing the cornflour with around 3–4 tablespoons of cold water in a small mug to make a runny paste. Add this to the slow cooker and stir well. Add the broccoli and stir once more before putting the lid back on and cooking for another 30–35 minutes on HIGH until the sauce has thickened and the broccoli has cooked.

Serve over noodles or rice with the extra 1 tablespoon of sesame seeds scattered over. Garnish with sliced spring onion, if you like.

No slow cooker? Cook the beef in the stock and seasonings on the hob in a lidded large saucepan over a low–medium heat for approximately 1½ hours or until it's tender. Add the cornflour slurry and broccoli and cook for a further 10–15 minutes until thickened and the broccoli is tender.

spag bol mac and cheese

This recipe combines spaghetti bolognese and macaroni cheese into one gorgeous meal that's creamy, cheesy and comforting – need I say more?!

 GF*

 EF

DF*

Serves 3 adults and 3 littles

Prep 10 minutes, Cook 2½–4½ hours

Freezable

Love your leftovers

Transfer leftovers to an ovenproof dish immediately to stop the cooking process, and prepare for turning them into a pasta bake. Keep in the fridge for up to 2 days. Reheat in the oven at 200°C fan (220°C/425°F/Gas 7), with a little extra cheese on top, and bake until piping hot. You can also freeze leftovers for up to 2 months. Defrost thoroughly and then reheat as above or in the microwave for 2–3 minutes on HIGH.

500g (1lb 2oz) lean minced (ground) beef
2 large carrots
500g (1lb 2oz) passata (strained tomatoes)
2 tbsp tomato purée (paste)
650ml (2¾ cups) milk*

1 tsp dried porcini mushroom powder (optional)
1 low-salt beef stock cube*, crumbled
1 tsp Dijon mustard
1 tsp garlic granules
2 tsp smoked paprika
2 tsp dried mixed herbs

350g (3⅓ cups) dried macaroni pasta*
150g (5½oz) Cheddar cheese*, grated
100g (½ cup) cream cheese*
freshly ground black pepper

Set a large, non-stick frying pan over a high heat to warm up. When the pan is hot, add the beef and break it up using a wooden spoon. Cook for 4–5 minutes until browned. Try to avoid touching the meat too much as it cooks so that it has lots of contact with the hot pan and gains some caramelized bits, as this is where the flavour is.

In the meantime, wash, then finely dice or coarsely grate the carrots – no need to peel them as there's lots of goodness in the skin. Add the carrots to the slow cooker along with the passata, tomato purée, half of the milk, the mushroom powder, if using, crumbled stock cube, Dijon mustard, garlic granules, paprika, mixed herbs and plenty of black pepper.

Add the beef once it's browned and stir well. Pop the lid on the slow cooker and cook on HIGH for 2 hours or on LOW for 4 hours.

Now remove the lid, add the rest of the milk and the macaroni pasta. Stir really well, cover and cook for a further 20–40 minutes on LOW, or until the pasta is cooked. The time really depends on your pasta and your slow cooker – it should soften quickly and easily, so taste to check the texture after 20 minutes and if it's not done, give it another 10 minutes, then check again. Once the pasta is soft, add the Cheddar cheese and cream cheese, stir and allow to stand for a few moments before serving.

No slow cooker? Follow the same steps as above, but cook the whole lot in a non-stick saucepan over a medium heat for 30 minutes, stirring often, then for another 10–15 minutes once the rest of the milk and the pasta have been added until the pasta is tender.

sweet and sour pork

Make your own fakeaway at home with this popular, gloriously flavoursome Chinese dish. Many traditional recipes use a lot of added sugar to achieve that sweet element, but this version uses pineapple juice for a healthier option, making it suitable for all ages.

 GF*
 EF
 V*
 DF

Serves 3 adults and 2 littles

Prep 10 minutes, Cook 3–6 hours

Freezable

Love your leftovers

Leftovers will keep for up to 2–3 days in an airtight container in the fridge. Reheat in the microwave on HIGH for 2-3 minutes, or over a gentle heat in a saucepan until piping hot. Leftovers will also freeze for up to 3 months. Defrost thoroughly before reheating as above.

1 tbsp garlic-infused oil
approx. 700g (1lb 9oz) diced pork shoulder*
2 tbsp cornflour (cornstarch)

Sauce
1 red pepper, deseeded and roughly chopped
1 yellow pepper, deseeded and roughly chopped

1 onion, cut into quarter chunks
2 garlic cloves, crushed
3 tbsp low-salt and low-sugar tomato ketchup
3 tbsp apple cider vinegar
1 x 435g (15oz) can of pineapple chunks in juice

2 tbsp low-salt soy sauce*
1 tbsp maple syrup (optional)
1½ tbsp cornflour (cornstarch)

Set a large, non-stick frying pan over a high heat on the hob. Add the garlic oil and let it heat up until very hot.

Coat the diced pork in the cornflour in the open packet the meat came in to save washing up.

Add the pork to the hot frying pan and spread the chunks into an even single layer – you may need to do this in 2 batches to avoid overcrowding the pan, which will make the pork stew rather than fry. Cook for 3 minutes without touching the pan to get some nice colour on the outside of the pork, then toss and cook for a further 1–2 minutes until browned all over.

Meanwhile, make the sauce. Add the chopped peppers and onion to the slow cooker, followed by 200ml (scant 1 cup) of cold water, the crushed garlic cloves, tomato ketchup, apple cider vinegar, the can of pineapple chunks along with the juice, soy sauce and maple syrup, if using.

Meat swaps
If you want an alternative to pork, you can swap it for diced chicken thighs or stewing steak (beef). Root veggies like butternut squash also work, however, don't use maple syrup if you choose this option as they are already sweet. The veggies won't need to be seared in the pan first.

In a separate small bowl or mug, mix the cornflour with a small splash of cold water from the tap to form a thin paste, then pour this into the slow cooker too.

Add the browned meat to the slow cooker. Stir very well before popping the lid on and cooking on HIGH for 3 hours or LOW for 4–6 hours.

Serve over rice or noodles. Turn to the next page to see how it looks.

No slow cooker? Brown the meat in the oil in a large casserole pot, then add all the remaining ingredients and simmer with the lid on over a low heat on the hob for 1–2 hours, or until the pork is tender.

hodgepodge shortcut lasagne

Italian traditionalists, please look away now! This throw-it-together dish tastes like an oven-baked layered lasagne, but the cooking method is a lot simpler. It looks a little scruffier, but saves you time cutting everything up for the little ones.

 GF*

 EF

 DF*

Serves 3 adults and 2 littles

Prep 10 minutes, Cook 2–3 hours

Freezable

Love your leftovers

This dish is best served fresh, however, leftovers will keep for up to 2 days in the fridge. They can be reheated in a hot oven for around 20 minutes with an extra splash of water. You can also freeze leftovers for up to 2 months. Reheat from frozen for around 35 minutes until piping hot throughout.

1 tbsp garlic-infused oil
500g (1lb 2oz) minced beef (5–10% fat)
500g (1lb 2oz) passata (strained tomatoes)
2 x 400g (14oz) cans of chopped tomatoes
3 tsp garlic purée

2 tsp dried mixed herbs
2 heaped tsp smoked paprika
250g (1 cup) ricotta cheese*
250g (1 cup) mascarpone cheese*
50ml (¼ cup) milk*

2 tbsp tomato purée (paste)
300g (10½oz) fresh lasagne sheets*
80g (2¾oz) Cheddar cheese*, grated
freshly ground black pepper

Set a large, non-stick frying pan over the highest heat on the hob and let it heat up. Add the garlic oil to the pan, followed by the beef. Use a wooden spoon to break up the meat, then leave it alone for 2 minutes to cook.

While the meat is cooking, add the passata and cans of chopped tomatoes to the slow cooker, along with 2 teaspoons of the garlic purée, the dried herbs, smoked paprika and black pepper to taste.

Give the mince a stir, breaking up any lumps. Cook for a further 2 minutes.

Meanwhile, add the ricotta, mascarpone, the remaining teaspoon of garlic purée and the milk to a medium bowl. Stir together well, then set aside.

Add the tomato purée to the browned mince and cook, stirring, for 1 minute. Tip the meat into the slow cooker and stir thoroughly.

For all but one of the lasagne sheets, scrumple them up in your hands to break them into small pieces, then add to the slow cooker. Stir well to submerge the pasta in the sauce, ensuring it's evenly spread around the whole pot. Lay the remaining whole lasagne sheet on top of everything in the middle, then spread over the ricotta and mascarpone sauce, reaching right to the edges. Sprinkle the grated cheese on top. Lay several sheets of kitchen paper over the top of the slow cooker pot to soak up excess moisture and pop the lid on over the top. Pull the paper so it is taught under the lid and not flopping down into the food. Cook on LOW for around 2–3 hours, or until the pasta is soft. If you want a crispy top, you can brown the lasagne (minus the kitchen paper) under the grill, if your slow cooker pot allows it.

Allow to stand for 10 minutes before serving alongside a refreshing salad.

No slow cooker? Brown the beef, then add the tomatoes and seasonings to your frying pan and cook for 10 minutes. Add this to a large, ovenproof dish, before stirring in the lasagne pieces and topping with the whole lasagne sheet, white sauce and grated cheese. Bake in an oven preheated to 200°C fan (220°C/425°F/Gas 7) for around 30 minutes.

Tingle those taste buds
To ramp up the flavour, when frying the mince, crumble a low-salt beef stock cube into the pan and add a teaspoon of sugar to the tomato sauce.

Store cupboard staple
You can use dried pasta sheets (instead of fresh), but you'll need to add a good splash of water to the sauce to make sure the pasta cooks through.

turkish chicken stew

This dish is one to cook when it's a little miserable outside, the kids are playing and you have 10 minutes to prep dinner. Then you can enjoy those delicious smells coming from the kitchen for the whole afternoon. There's soft potatoes, tender chicken and chunks of courgette and aubergine which just melt into the sauce, so any picky eaters may be fooled of their presence completely.

 GF*

 EF

 DF

Serves 2 adults and 2 littles

Prep 10 minutes, Cook 4–7 hours

Freezable

Love your leftovers

Leftovers will keep in the fridge for up to 2 days. Reheat in a saucepan until everything is piping hot throughout, especially the chicken. You can also freeze the stew for up to 3 months. Defrost at room temperature before reheating as above.

1 low-salt chicken stock cube*
700g (1lb 9oz) all-rounder potatoes
1 large courgette (zucchini)
1 large aubergine (eggplant)
3 tsp sweet paprika
2 tsp ground turmeric
2 tsp minced or crushed garlic
1½ tsp ground cumin
1½ tsp dried oregano
6 boneless, skinless chicken thighs
freshly ground black pepper

Crumble the stock cube into a jug, then add 600ml (2½ cups) of boiling water from the kettle. Stir until the stock cube has dissolved, then set aside.

Peel the potatoes and cut them into approx. 2cm (¾in) cubes. Using a vegetable peeler, peel the courgette, then cut it into battons. Chop each batton into approx. 1.5cm (⅝in) chunks. Using a paring knife (because it's a little tricky using the veg peeler), remove the skin of the aubergine as thinly as you can, trying to avoid removing any of the white flesh. Chop the aubergine up into the same size pieces as the courgette.

Add all the chopped veggies to the slow cooker along with the paprika, turmeric, garlic, cumin, oregano and a little black pepper. Add the whole chicken thighs, unfolding them if they have been bunched up inside the packet. Pour the stock into the slow cooker pot and give everything a really good stir.

Pop the lid on and cook on HIGH for 4 hours or on LOW for 6–7 hours, or until the chicken is tender and falls apart easily.

Serve in big bowls, with a little bread for dipping, if you wish. This dish is delicious as it is, but adults may prefer a little salt on their portion to bring out the flavours even more.

No slow cooker? Dissolve the stock cube in the same way as above, then add this along with the remaining ingredients to a lidded casserole pot, cover and bake at 170°C fan (190°C/375°F/Gas 5) for 1–1½ hours, or until the chicken and veggies are tender.

Serving to little ones
You can either serve this dish chunky or mash the veggies and potato into the flavourful sauce to enjoy on a spoon.

easy aubergine stew

This satisfying aubergine stew has smoky, nutty flavour vibes, which remind me of a traditional baba ganoush dip. Serve with rice, bread for dunking or coated over pasta – delicious!

 GF*
 EF
 V*
 Vg*
 DF

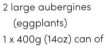

Serves 2 adults and 2 littles

Prep 10 minutes, Cook 4 –7 hours

Freezable

Love your leftovers

Leftovers will keep for up to 2 days in the fridge. Reheat in a saucepan, with an extra splash of water if needed, until piping hot throughout. The stew will also keep in the freezer for up to 3 months. Defrost and then reheat as above.

2 large aubergines (eggplants)
1 x 400g (14oz) can of crushed tomatoes
1 low-salt vegetable or chicken stock cube*
1 tsp sugar or honey* for over 1's (optional)
1 tbsp tomato purée (paste)
2 tsp dried mixed herbs
15g (½oz) dried porcini mushrooms
2 tsp ground cumin
2 tsp smoked paprika
1 tsp sesame oil
sesame seeds, to serve (optional)
a little freshly ground black pepper

I find this dish is best if you peel the aubergines, but it's not necessary. To peel, I recommend using a sharp paring knife to very thinly slice the skin off the outside, being careful to avoid removing too much of the aubergine flesh. Whether you've peeled them or not, cut the aubergines into cubes, approx. 2cm (¾in) in size – no need to be precise as we'll mash it all later.

Add the cubed aubergine to the slow cooker, followed by the can of tomatoes. Fill up the empty can with cold tap water and swill it round to catch any remaining tomato, then add this to the slow cooker too. Crumble the stock cube into the slow cooker, before adding all the remaining ingredients, apart from the sesame oil and sesame seeds. Give it all a really good stir, then press all the aubergine chunks down into the liquid and pop the lid on the slow cooker. Cook on HIGH for 4 hours, or LOW for 6–7 hours.

Once the stew is done and the aubergine is super tender, add the sesame oil and use a potato masher to break down the chunks of aubergine (as pictured in the small bowl). Stir everything together so that the mashed aubergine gives the stew a thick, luscious consistency. Or you can leave it chunky if you prefer (as pictured in the larger bowl). Serve with a sprinkling of sesame seeds if you wish.

If serving to little ones, note that even though the dried mushrooms will have rehydrated and softened, babas may still find them tricky to chew, so you can remove these from their portion. Alternatively, pop their portion onto a clean chopping board and run a sharp knife over it, or whizz in a food processor.

No slow cooker? Add all the ingredients to a saucepan, cover and simmer over a low heat on the hob for approx. 30–40 minutes, until the aubergine is tender. Mash or blend with a stick blender and add the sesame oil and seeds to finish.

slow cooker mushroom ragù

A meat-free dinner option with deep, rich umami flavours that are intensified through slow cooking. Because the mushrooms have been grated and slowly cooked, they melt into the sauce making it perfect for little taste testers.

Serves 2 adults and 3 littles

Prep 8 minutes, Cook 3½–6 hours

Freezable

♡

Love your leftovers

Leftovers will keep for up to 3 days in the fridge. Reheat in a saucepan or in the microwave on HIGH for 2–3 minutes until piping hot. This dish can also be frozen for up to 4 months. Defrost, then reheat as above.

2 low-salt vegetable or chicken stock cubes*
500g (1lb 2oz) chestnut mushrooms, wiped clean
1 large brown onion

500g (1lb 2oz) passata (strained tomatoes)
2 tbsp tomato purée (paste)
2 tsp dried mixed herbs
2 tbsp Worcestershire sauce* (optional)

10–15g (¼–½oz) dried porcini mushrooms
2 tsp dried porcini mushroom powder (optional)
a little freshly ground black pepper

Fill the kettle with water and put it on to boil.

Crumble the stock cubes into a jug, then pour over 400ml (1⅔ cups) of boiling water from the kettle, stirring to dissolve.

Coarsely grate the mushrooms and onion using a box grater or the grater attachment in a food processor, which will be much quicker.

Add the grated vegetable pulp to the slow cooker pot along with the stock and the rest of the ingredients. If your dried mushroom pieces are very large, use kitchen scissors or a sharp knife to chop them down to 1cm (½in) pieces before adding.

Pop the lid on the slow cooker and cook for 3½ hours on HIGH or 5–6 hours on LOW (it can actually bubble away on LOW for a bit longer if needed).

Serve with freshly cooked pasta or on jacket potatoes for a warming and comforting family meal.

No slow cooker? Add all the ingredients to a saucepan and cook with the lid on over a medium–low heat for 30–40 minutes. If it's looking too dry, add a touch more water, or if it looks a little watery, take the lid off and allow the sauce to reduce to your desired consistency.

slow cooker beef korma

My version of this classic has extra veg grated in the sauce. The little ones won't know it's there, but it adds a yummy flavour and an extra bit of nutrition. What I love about a korma is that it involves ground nuts, which are packed full of healthy fats and vitamins.

 GF*
 EF
 V*
 DF*

Serves 3 adults and 3 littles

Prep 10 minutes, Cook 3–6 hours

Freezable

Love your leftovers

Leftovers will keep for up to 3 days in the fridge or freeze for up to 2 months. Reheat in the microwave on HIGH from chilled or in a saucepan until piping hot. Or blast in the microwave from frozen for 3–4 minutes until fully defrosted and piping hot throughout.

1 tbsp sunflower oil
600–800g (1lb 5oz–1lb 12oz) diced stewing beef* (see note)
1 low-salt chicken or veggie stock cube*
1 large onion
2 courgettes (zucchini)
150ml (⅔ cup) plain yogurt or double (heavy) cream*
60g (⅔ cup) ground almonds
2 garlic cloves, crushed
2 tsp ginger purée
2 tbsp tomato purée (paste)
2 tsp mild curry powder
2 tsp garam masala (a mild blend)
1 tsp ground turmeric
1 tsp ground cumin
1 tsp sugar (optional)
freshly ground black pepper
coriander (cilantro), to serve (optional)

Set a large frying pan over a high heat and add the sunflower oil. Fill your kettle and put it on to boil.

Add the meat to the hot pan and cook for 2–3 minutes, tossing once or twice, until browned. If your frying pan is small, do this in two batches.

Meanwhile, crumble the stock cube into a jug. Pour over 250ml (generous 1 cup) of boiling water from the kettle, stir to dissolve and set aside.

Grate the onion and courgettes on a box grater, or use a food processor to pulse until finely chopped. Add these to the slow cooker along with any juices, the yogurt or cream and ground almonds.

Tip the browned meat into the slow cooker, then place the pan with the meat juices over the heat. Add the garlic and ginger and tomato purées and cook for 30–60 seconds. Add the curry powder, garam masala, turmeric, cumin and some black pepper. Stir and cook for 30 seconds more.

Pour in the stock and deglaze the frying pan by using a wooden spoon to scrape up any lumps stuck to the bottom. Pour the liquid from the pan into the slow cooker, add the sugar, if using, then give it all a good stir. Place the lid on the slow cooker and cook on LOW for 6 hours or HIGH for 3–4 hours.

Once the meat is tender, give the korma a stir – if it looks slightly separated don't worry, it just needs stirring together. Serve with rice or flatbreads and fresh coriander, if you like. Plus a little seasoning for the adult portions.

No slow cooker? Brown the meat in a large casserole pot and remove it to a plate before sautéing the onion until soft in a little more oil. Add the spices, garlic, ginger and tomato purée and cook for a further few moments before adding the stock and yogurt or cream, almonds, the browned meat, veg and sugar. Cover with the lid and simmer over a low heat for 2–3 hours. Or, cook in an oven preheated to 160°C fan (180°C/350°F/Gas 4) for 2–3 hours.

Meat swaps
This korma can also be
made with diced chicken
thighs or breast, diced lamb
shoulder or diced root veg
like butternut squash. Use the
same quantities, however, if
you're using veg there is no
need to brown it in the pan
beforehand.

sweet potato and chickpea curry

Incredibly easy to throw together, this is a bung-it-all-in-the-pot kinda recipe. With protein-packed chickpeas and a sweet, creamy, mildly spiced flavour, this veg-packed curry is great for both little ones and adults.

Serves 2 adults and 3 littles

Prep 8 minutes, Cook 4–8 hours

Freezable

Love your leftovers

Leftovers will keep for up to 3 days in the fridge, or freeze for up to 4 months. To reheat from chilled or defrosted, place in a saucepan until bubbling. You can also microwave the curry from frozen for 3–5 minutes on HIGH until piping hot throughout.

1kg (2lb 4oz) sweet potatoes
1 brown onion, finely diced or grated
1 x 400g (14oz) can of crushed tomatoes
1 x 400g (14oz) can of coconut milk
1 x 400g (15oz) can of chickpeas in water, drained
1 tbsp mild curry powder
1 tbsp mild garam masala
2 tsp ground turmeric
2 tsp minced fresh garlic or garlic granules
2 tsp finely grated fresh ginger (optional)
6 cubes of frozen spinach
a good grinding of black pepper

Peel the sweet potatoes and roughly chop them into 2.5cm (1in) chunks. Add these to the slow cooker along with the rest of the ingredients.

Fill the empty tomato can a quarter of the way with cold tap water, swill it round to catch any tomato residue and add this to the slow cooker pot too. Stir well, place the lid on the slow cooker and cook for 4 hours on HIGH or 7–8 hours on LOW until the sweet potatoes are very soft.

If you prefer a less chunky texture, use a potato masher to roughly mash all the potato chunks until you can't see any large lumps, this will instantly thicken the curry. Serve over a bed of rice or with flatbreads for dunking. To help baby pick it up and enjoy their meal independently, you can try serving the rice mixed with curry on a spoon, or form into rough balls by squishing it together in your hands. Adults feel free to add a dash of hot chilli sauce to your portion and a sprinkling of salt, if you desire.

Got an extra minute? To intensify the curry flavour, whilst you peel the spuds, sauté the onion in a frying pan with a touch of oil until soft and translucent. Add the spices and cook for 30–60 seconds, taking care not to let them burn, before adding the tomatoes. Frying spices like this releases their flavour even more. Add the spiced tomatoes to the slow cooker with the remaining ingredients and cook as above.

No slow cooker? Sauté the onion in a little oil in a large casserole pot before adding the spices and aromatics. Cook for 30–60 seconds to release the flavours, before adding the remaining ingredients. Cover and simmer on the hob for around 1 hour or until the sweet potato is falling apart.

courgette and tomato risotto

With this one you simply throw it all in and give it a good stir at the end. Risotto has never been so easy!

GF*
EF
V*
Vg*
DF*

Serves 3 adults and 2 littles

Prep 8 minutes, Cook 1½– 3 hours

Freezable

Love your leftovers

Leftovers will keep for up to 24 hours in the fridge or 3 months in the freezer. If you plan to keep some, immediately spread the leftover risotto out onto a cold plate to help it cool quickly so that it's at a safe temperature for storing. Once cool, scoop into an airtight container and chill or freeze straight away. Defrost in the fridge overnight if needed, then reheat in a saucepan with a splash of water until piping hot.

2 low-salt chicken or vegetable stock cubes*

1 large courgette (zucchini)

1 onion

300g (1½ cups) risotto rice

1 tsp garlic granules

1 x 400g (14oz) can of good-quality cherry tomatoes

2 tbsp unsalted butter*

80g (2¾oz) Cheddar cheese*, grated

50g (¼ cup) cream cheese*

freshly ground black pepper

Put the kettle on to boil. Crumble the stock cubes into a jug, then fill it with 1 litre (4¼ cups) of boiling water. Stir to dissolve the stock cubes.

Lightly grease the inside of the slow cooker pot to avoid the rice sticking. Coarsely grate the courgette and onion on a box grater or using the grater attachment on a food processor. Add the grated veg to the slow cooker along with the stock, risotto rice, garlic granules and a little black pepper. Add the can of cherry tomatoes, then quarter-fill the empty can with cold tap water and swill out any remaining tomato juice, adding this to the slow cooker too.

Stir well, put the lid on cook for 1½–2½ hours on HIGH. The time really depends on the size and power of your slow cooker. Check after about an hour, then at 30-minute intervals by giving it a good stir and having a taste of the rice when it's starting to look done. If the rice doesn't taste grainy or crunchy and the majority of the water has been absorbed, then it's done. If it needs more cooking, add a touch more boiling water if it's looking dry, and cook for a further 20–30 minutes before checking again.

Once done, add the butter, Cheddar cheese and cream cheese and stir to melt them into the risotto. They will transform the consistency of the dish to make it super creamy.

Serve with a side salad and extra seasoning for the adults, if you wish.

No slow cooker? Add all the ingredients to a large, non-stick saucepan, stir well, cover and simmer over a gentle heat on the hob until the rice is cooked. It won't need stirring, but check on it every now and then to ensure the liquid hasn't totally evaporated before the rice is cooked, in which case you can top up the pan with a splash of boiling water.

creamy butternut squash pasta

A veg-packed meal that is so simple to throw together. Even the fussiest eaters will love it.

 GF*
 EF
 V*
 Vg*
 DF*

Serves 2 hungry adults and 3 littles

Prep 10 minutes, Cook 3½–6½ hours

Freezable

Love your leftovers

Leftovers will keep for up to 2 days in the fridge or freeze for up to 3 months. The pasta will keep cooking in the hot slow cooker, so decant leftovers into a bowl to stop the cooking process. It will also thicken once cool, so add a splash of milk when reheating. To reheat, either cook until piping hot in a pan, or pop in the microwave on HIGH for 2–3 minutes. If frozen, defrost thoroughly and reheat as above.

1 large butternut squash, peeled, deseeded and roughly chopped (approx. 800g–1kg/ 1lb 12oz–2lb 4oz chopped weight)

1 onion, roughly chopped

3 large garlic cloves, roughly chopped

1 low-salt chicken or vegetable stock cube*

220g (7¾oz) dried pasta of your choice*

200ml (scant 1 cup) milk*

100g (½ cup) cream cheese*

90g (3¼oz) smoked Cheddar cheese*, grated

2 tsp smoked paprika freshly ground black pepper

Boil the kettle.

Add the chopped butternut squash, onion and garlic to your slow cooker along with a generous grinding of black pepper. Crumble in the stock cube, then add 500ml (generous 2 cups) of boiling water from the kettle. Stir to dissolve the stock cube, then pop the lid on and cook on HIGH for 3 hours or LOW for 5–6 hours until the veg is very tender.

Once it's ready, blend the veg and cooking liquid to a very smooth purée, either with a stick blender or decant into a food processor, then pour back into the slow cooker. The mixture you have is now essentially butternut squash soup, which you can always thin down to your desired consistency and serve as it is if you'd like.

Today we're making pasta, so add the uncooked pasta, the milk, cream cheese, grated smoked cheese and smoked paprika to the butternut squash purée and stir well. Place the lid back on the slow cooker and cook for a further 30–40 minutes on LOW, or until the pasta is cooked.

Serve this up as it is. Adults, feel free to add a touch of salt and pepper to your portions.

This dish is also fantastic the next day as a pasta bake. Simply pour into an oven dish with a splash more milk, top with extra grated cheese and bake at 200°C fan (220°C/425°F/Gas 7) for around 20 minutes, or until the cheese is crisp and golden on top.

No slow cooker? Boil the squash in the stock in a large saucepan with the garlic and onion over a medium heat on the hob for 20 minutes until tender, then blend. Meanwhile, boil the pasta in a separate pan, then combine with the squash purée, smoked cheese, cream cheese, paprika and black pepper. Use as much milk as you require for thinning down the sauce.

slow cooker fruity crumble

There are lots of reasons why a slow cooker is great, and this comforting fruity crumble has to be one of the most surprising. Soft, melt-in-the-mouth fruit topped with a crumbly, almost crisp in parts, topping. It's absolutely glorious with a dash of custard or cream!

 GF*

 EF

 V

 Vg*

 DF*

Serves 3 adults and 2 littles

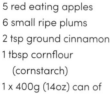

Prep 10 minutes, Cook 3–6 hours

Freezable

Love your leftovers

Leftovers will keep for up to 2–3 days in the fridge or 3 months in the freezer. Defrost in the fridge. To reheat, spoon into an ovenproof dish, trying to keep the fruit at the bottom and the crumble on top, then bake for 15 minutes at 180°C fan (200°C/400°F/ Gas 6). until piping hot. Alternatively, you can blast it in the microwave for 60–90 seconds on HIGH, but this will give a soggier finish.

5 red eating apples
6 small ripe plums
2 tsp ground cinnamon
1 tbsp cornflour (cornstarch)
1 x 400g (14oz) can of peach slices in

unsweetened fruit juice
150g (scant 1½ cups) rolled porridge oats*
80g (⅔ cup) plain (all-purpose) flour*
1 tsp vanilla extract

90g (generous ⅓ cup) unsalted butter*, melted
40g (scant ¼ cup) light soft brown sugar (optional)

Peel, core and cut the apples into approx. 2cm (¾in) wide wedges and add these to the slow cooker. Halve the plums and remove the stones, then cut them into quarters and add to the apples. Sprinkle the cinnamon and cornflour over the fruit, then stir well to coat the fruit evenly. Pour the entire can of peach slices and their juice over the fruit and stir again.

In a separate bowl, mix together the oats, flour, vanilla extract, melted butter and brown sugar, if using, until you see no dry oats or flour. Evenly sprinkle the crumble mixture over the fruit, reaching right to the edges of the slow cooker pot.

Take four sheets of fragrance-free kitchen paper and place them over the top of the slow cooker pot in a double layer, using more paper if you see any gaps. Place the lid on the slow cooker over the paper. Gently pull the paper so it is fairly taught under the lid and not flopping down into the crumble. The job of this paper is to soak up as much condensation as possible, which should stop the crumble topping from going soggy.

Cook on HIGH for 3 hours or LOW for 5–6 hours, until the fruit is soft and the crumble topping is crisp. Be careful when you take the lid off as there will be lots of water droplets on it, so quickly move the lid away from the slow cooker to avoid the water dripping back down into the crumble and remove the kitchen paper. If you're at home, you can replace the kitchen paper with fresh sheets halfway through cooking if the pieces of paper sticking out seem saturated. However, don't worry if this isn't convenient, it will be totally fine if you don't replace them.

Serve the warm crumble in bowls with a dash of custard or cream.

No slow cooker? This crumble will cook perfectly well as a traditional pud in the oven. I recommend using fridge-cold cubed butter instead of melted, and rubbing it into the oats and flour for the crispiest topping.

Out of kitchen paper?
If you don't have any kitchen paper, you can use a clean, dry tea towel instead. Just ensure you haven't used a strong smelling fabric conditioner, as this will seep into the crumble and give it a funny taste.

hot mulled apple juice

The glee in my 4-year-old's face as I handed her a warm cup of this cinnamon-infused, comforting drink. "Oh my goodness mummy, did you really make this? It's so good!" Well, that's what any parent wants to hear, right?

 GF
 EF
 V
 Vg
 DF

Makes approx. 6 adult-size mugs

Cook in 2–3 hours

Freezable

Love your leftovers

This juice will keep for up to 2–3 days in the fridge. I recommend straining it into a jug to store so that the flavour doesn't become too strong as it sits. You can serve it cold, dilute with a little fizzy water or reheat in the microwave or in a saucepan on the hob. You can also make ice pops out of leftovers and keep them in the freezer for up to 6 months.

900ml (3¾ cups) fresh unsweetened apple juice, not from concentrate

700ml (3 cups) tap water
1 cinnamon stick

3 red crisp eating apples (optional but adds extra flavour)
1 small orange

Add the apple juice, water and cinnamon stick to the slow cooker. If you are using them, cut the apples into wedges and discard the cores – no need to peel in my opinion. Add these to the slow cooker too.

Use a potato peeler to peel the zest off the orange, taking care to only peel the orange zest and not the white pith attached, as this will make the juice a little bitter. Add the zest to the slow cooker and squeeze the juice of the orange in too, catching any pips in your hands as you do.

Pop the lid on and cook on HIGH for 2–3 hours until hot and smelling delicious. Strain the liquid into mugs to serve. Add a dash of cold water to cool it down for the little ones.

The apples stewed in the juice are delicious served warm over ice cream, or save them for breakfast in the morning to top porridge. Alternatively, mash them well and use them to make the Cinnamon Apple Toast (see page 22).

Note The fruit juice in this recipe has been diluted with water, however, I still recommend serving it alongside something to eat so any natural sugars don't sit on the teeth for too long. This rule applies when serving all fruit juices. If you're serving to under 2s, feel free to dilute the juice further with water and serve in moderation.

No slow cooker? Add all the ingredients to a large saucepan and simmer for approx. 20–30 minutes on the hob until the flavours have infused.

no cook

When the kids want something simple, or you don't fancy getting the pots and pans out, try these quick and easy recipes to feed the family. They're also great for packed lunches in a hurry or simple supper out in the garden on a warm summer's evening!

strawberry cottage cheesecake bowls

Whether for breakfast, part of a picky lunch or served as dessert, this comforting dish will please the whole gang.

 GF*

 EF

 V

 Vg*

 DF*

Makes 4 large bowls

Prep 5 minutes, Setting time 30 minutes+

Freezable

Love your leftovers

These can be stored for up to 2–3 days in the fridge, so you can keep popping back for more as and when needed. You can also freeze them to be enjoyed as a kind of frozen yogurt, however, please note that they will not defrost to the same texture as before.

160g (5¾oz) fresh ripe strawberries, plus extra for decorating
300ml (1¼ cups) cottage cheese* or dairy-free cream cheese

200g (1 cup) thick Greek yogurt*
1 tbsp alcohol-free vanilla extract
40g (¼ cup) chia seeds

30g (⅛ cup) maple syrup or honey* for over 1's (optional)
4–6 Nutty Oat Cookies* (see page 104) or shop-bought cookies (optional)

Mash the strawberries in a bowl with a fork or blitz them to a purée in a food processor, then transfer to a bowl.

Add the cottage cheese (or your alternative), plus the yogurt, vanilla extract, chia seeds and maple syrup or honey, if using. Stir until all the ingredients are very well combined.

Crumble 1–2 oat biscuits in your hand into the base of each serving bowl. This is completely optional, but it adds a lovely variety in texture to the dish. Spoon the cottage cheese mixture on top, followed by a few extra fresh strawberries for decoration.

Pop the dishes in the fridge for at least 30 minutes until the cheesecakes are set, then enjoy.

Note My family love the cottage cheese curds in this thick, creamy, pudding-like dish, however, if you're not keen, replace the amount of cottage cheese with 50/50 cream cheese and milk.

chocolate and banana breakfast milkshake

With fruits, protein and carbs all in one glass, this balanced drink will fill you up and keep the kiddos happy.

 GF*

 EF

 V

 Vg*

 DF*

**Serves 1 adult
and 1 little**

**Prep
4 minutes**

Freezable

**Love your
leftovers**

This milkshake will keep for up to 2 days, covered, in the fridge. If you have plenty left that won't get drunk in time, you can make ice pops with the leftovers. Pour into ice lolly moulds and freeze until solid. Enjoy as a cool breakfast on a hot summer's day.

1 large ripe banana
2–3 tsp unsweetened cocoa powder

4 heaped tsp of your favourite unsweetened yogurt*

4 tbsp rolled porridge oats*
220ml (1 cup) milk of your choice*

Add all the ingredients to a blender pot and whizz until super smooth. The oats will feel a touch lumpy in the mixture. My family don't mind this, however, you can let it stand for 5 minutes to allow the oats to soften and then blend again for a smoother consistency. Pour into glasses or cups, or serve to little ones in a small bowl with a spoon.

Don't fancy chocolate? Swap the cocoa powder for a handful of your favourite fresh berries. Raspberries, blueberries and strawberries all work really well here. Or try a handful of frozen fruit if you have it.

overnight oats

There is nothing more satisfying than waking up to a ready-made breakfast! We enjoy these overnight oats cold, but you can also heat them in the microwave for 1–2 minutes until piping hot for a warm start to the day. Feel free to add a little maple syrup or honey for over 1s if you have a sweet tooth. Turn to pages 204–205 to see how these recipes look.

gingerbread

Serves 1 adult and 1 little

Prep 5 minutes, Chill for 3 hours or overnight

Freezable

This is a great one to have in the colder months as it's spiced with warming flavours.

1 ripe banana
100g (1 cup) rolled porridge oats*

220ml (1 cup) milk of your choice*
½ tsp ground ginger

1 tsp ground cinnamon

Mash the banana in a small bowl, then add the remaining ingredients and stir well.

Cover and keep in the fridge for a minimum of 3 hours or overnight.

GF*
EF
V
Vg*
DF*

cinnamon and clementine

Using canned fruit gives a really delicious sweetness to this combo.

1 x 300g (10½oz) can of clementine or mandarin segments in fruit juice

1 tsp ground cinnamon
100g (1 cup) rolled porridge oats*

140ml (scant ⅔ cup) milk of your choice*
1 tsp alcohol-free vanilla extract

Add the entire can of fruit, including the juice, to a small bowl. Add the rest of the ingredients and stir well.

Cover and keep in the fridge for a minimum of 3 hours or overnight.

GF*
EF
V
Vg*
DF*

Love your leftovers

These will both keep well for up to 2–3 days in the fridge. Add more milk if the oats have thickened too much. You can also freeze them for up to 2 months. Defrost, then enjoy cold or heat up with an extra splash of milk (see recipe intro).

mango, raspberry and coconut

Naturally sweet and dairy-free with tropical vibes, this is fab for a warm morning.

60g (2oz) fresh or frozen raspberries
150g (5½oz) frozen mango
30g (scant ½ cup) unsweetened desiccated (dried shredded) coconut
1 tsp alcohol-free vanilla extract
80g (generous ¾ cup) rolled porridge oats*
130g (⅔ cup) unsweetened dairy-free coconut yogurt
100ml (scant ½ cup) coconut milk, or any of your choice*

If using fresh raspberries, add the raspberries to a small bowl and crush them slightly with a spoon. Add all the remaining ingredients and stir well. Cover and keep in the fridge for a minimum of 3 hours or overnight.

If using frozen raspberries, just mix all the ingredients together and lightly crush the raspberries when they are soft in the morning.

chocolate and peanut butter

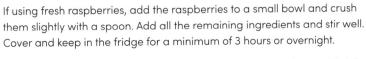

Comforting is the word to describe this bowl of deliciousness. The kids will love it!

1 ripe banana
10g (4 tsp) unsweetened cocoa powder
200ml (scant 1 cup) milk
of your choice*
70g (¾ cup) rolled porridge oats*
20g (1½ tbsp) chia seeds
50g (scant ¼ cup) crunchy or smooth peanut butter (100% nuts)

Add the banana and cocoa powder to a bowl and mash them together with a fork. Add the milk and whisk with the fork until fully incorporated. Add the oats, chia seeds and peanut butter before stirring again well.

Cover and keep in the fridge for a minimum of 3 hours or overnight.

Serves 1 adult and 1 little

Prep 5 minutes, Chill for 3 hours or overnight

Freezable*

*Only the Chocolate and Peanut Butter.

Love your leftovers

These will both keep for up to 2–3 days in the fridge. Add more milk if the oats have thickened too much. You can also freeze the Chocolate and Peanut Butter one for up to 2 months (the Mango, Raspberry and Coconut oats do not freeze well). Defrost, then enjoy cold or heat up with an extra splash of milk (see recipe intro).

toast toppers

Not just fantastic spread over toast, these two speedy recipes are perfect for filling sandwiches, topping crackers or serving alongside a picky lunch for an easy go-to meal.

avo egg 'mayo'

Each recipe makes enough for 2 large sarnies

Prep 5 minutes each

Love your leftovers

Leftovers for both fillings will keep for up to 2–3 days in the fridge.

 GF
 EF*
 V
 DF*

I like to boil half a dozen eggs at the start of the week for snacks and quick picky meals. This is one fab way to use up the last of the boiled eggs. Swapping the mayo for the much healthier fat of avocado makes this dish more nutritious and gets in another of your 5 a day!

3–4 cold hard-boiled eggs* (see Simple Swaps, opposite)
1 large ripe avocado

2 tbsp Greek yogurt*
1 tsp garlic granules
a little squeeze of lemon juice (or more

if you plan to keep leftovers)
freshly ground black pepper

Peel and roughly chop the hard-boiled eggs, or alternatively, coarsely grate the eggs for a smoother finish. Halve the avocado, remove the pit and scoop out the flesh into a large bowl. Mash the avocado with the back of a fork until smooth, then add the yogurt, garlic granules, lemon juice and a little black pepper. Stir well before adding the chopped or grated eggs, then stir one final time until well combined. Serve on crackers or toast, in a sandwich or with a picky lunch of your choosing.

mackerel pâté

 GF
 EF
DF*

This is my go-to lunch when I don't have much in the fridge. When shopping for mackerel, the salt levels differ from brand to brand, so try to buy it with the lowest levels you can find.

approx. 170g (6oz) of drained canned mackerel in spring water or olive oil

4 tbsp Greek yogurt*
juice of 1 small lemon
1 tsp garlic paste

a little freshly ground black pepper
chopped fresh chives, to garnish (optional)

Drain the mackerel fillets and add them to a bowl. Mash them a little using the back of a fork, then add the remaining ingredients and mash together to your desired consistency. I prefer my pâté a little chunky, but you can go as smooth as you like. This can also be done in a food processor, if you prefer, to speed things up even more. Serve the mackerel pâté with crackers, on toast or in a sarnie for a delicious picky lunch or quick supper. Garnish with chopped fresh chives, if you like.

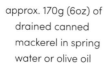

NO COOK

Simple swaps
To make it egg-free, switch the boiled eggs for mashed cannellini beans in the Avo Egg 'Mayo'. You can also swap mackerel out for canned tuna in the pâté, if you prefer.

cucumber sarnies two ways

I always feel very fancy eating a cucumber finger sandwich. It's a delicacy that's comprised of such simple flavours, but they really do work well together. Traditional recipes require you to salt the cucumber to draw out the moisture, with the aim of avoiding a soggy sarnie. This version skips the salt, instead simply squeezing the water out of grated cucumber, so that little ones can enjoy too.

Makes 12 finger sandwiches

¾ large cucumber
50g (¼ cup) cream cheese*

1 tbsp thick Greek yogurt* (if DF, swap the yogurt for extra DF cream cheese)
1 tsp garlic granules

8 soft slices of bread*
4 knobs (pats) of very soft unsalted butter*
freshly ground black pepper

Prep 8 minutes

Love your leftovers

If you do have leftovers, you can store them in an airtight container in the fridge for up to 24 hours.

Coarsely grate the cucumber using a box grater. Take handfuls of the grated cucumber pulp and squeeze them out as tightly as you can over the sink to remove excess liquid – a lot should come out. Add the dry cucumber to a clean bowl.

Add the cream cheese, yogurt, garlic granules and a little black pepper to the cucumber in the bowl and mix well.

Now you have two options for assembling these sarnies. Firstly, the traditional way: take two slices of bread and spread each one with a very thin layer of butter. Add around a tablespoon of the cucumber filling to one slice of buttered bread and spread it over from edge to edge. Place another piece of buttered bread on top, butter-side down. If you want to be super fancy, cut the crusts off, trying to remove as little of the soft bread as possible. Cut the sandwich into 3 finger strips along the short edge. Repeat with the remaining bread, butter and filling.

Your second option is to make some cucumber sandwich swirls: place a piece of bread on your chopping board and remove the crusts. With the palm of your hand, flatten the bread slightly, so that it still has a little bounce but is thinner. Spread with a thin layer of butter, before spreading over a tablespoon of the cucumber filling, reaching from edge-to-edge. From the short edge, roll the bread up into a sausage shape and then cut it widthways into 3–4 rounds. If you have spread the cucumber mixture right up to the edges, the spirals should stay together well. Repeat with the remaining bread, butter and filling.

Serve immediately for ultimate freshness.

Note If you fancy trying a different flavour, you can swap the cucumber for finely grated carrot.

hummus two ways

hummole

Makes approx. 500g (1lb 2oz)

Prep 5 minutes

Freezable

Love your leftovers

Both of these recipes will keep for up to 3–4 days tightly covered in the fridge, or freeze for up to 3 months. Defrost in the fridge and enjoy within 24 hours. For the Hummole, add an extra squeeze of lemon or lime juice to the top to prevent it from browning.

 GF
 EF
 V
 Vg
DF

I feel I need to apologise for this recipe name, I just couldn't help it. If you put guacamole and hummus together, you get this delicious creamy dip.

1 x 400g (15oz) can of chickpeas in water
1 large ripe avocado, halved and pitted
2 tsp sesame oil

1 garlic clove, roughly chopped
juice of 1 small lemon or lime

a small handful of fresh coriander (cilantro), optional
2 small salad tomatoes, roughly chopped

Open the can of chickpeas slightly and pour out most of the liquid, leaving a little behind. Add the contents of the can to a food processor, along with the avocado flesh, sesame oil, garlic and lemon or lime juice. Blend for 2–3 minutes until smooth. Taste the dip – it shouldn't taste grainy when it's ready. Add a splash of water, if needed, to help get the consistency silky.

Add the coriander, if using, and the tomatoes and pulse until the tomatoes are slightly blended into the dip, but still a bit chunky. If you prefer a smooth dip, blend for longer until they're fully combined. Serve with all your favourite dippers like veg sticks or bread sticks.

spiced hummus

 GF
 EF
 V
 Vg
DF

A traditional hummus with a spiced kick for extra flavour, this is perfect with vegetable sticks, pitta fingers or breadsticks.

1 x 400g (15oz) can of chickpeas in water, drained and rinsed
2 large garlic cloves, peeled
2 tsp smoked paprika

1½ tsp ground cumin
1 tsp mild garam masala
2 heaped tbsp tahini (100% sesame seed paste)

1 tbsp garlic-infused oil
juice of 1 lemon
a little freshly ground black pepper

Add all the ingredients to a food processor and blend until smooth.

Add a few dashes of boiling water out of the kettle (2–3 tablespoons) and blend again until the consistency is to your liking. I like to keep the food processor whizzing for around 2–3 minutes to make sure it's super creamy. Serve with your choice of veg sticks, pitta fingers and/or breadsticks.

Tip Try to get the best quality canned chickpeas you can afford, as these will give a more luxurious texture to your hummus. Tahini can separate when sitting in the fridge, so stir it well before using in the recipe.

quick dips

Each recipe makes 1 large sharing bowl

Both dips are ready in 5 minutes

Freezable

Love your leftovers

Both dips will keep in the fridge for up to 3–4 days or will freeze for up to 2 months. Defrost in the fridge and enjoy cold. You can also warm up any leftover pea purée, then stir through a handful of grated cheese before adding to cooked pasta for a simple meal.

tomato salsa

 GF

 EF

V

Vg

DF

A quick tomato salsa-style dip that's perfect for all the family.

2 large salad tomatoes
¼ red onion
½ large garlic clove
½ tsp dried mixed herbs
1 tsp tomato

purée (paste)
juice of ½ lime or lemon (optional)
1 tbsp garlic-infused oil
½ tsp sugar (optional)

handful of sweet cherry tomatoes (optional)
freshly ground black pepper

Finely grate the two large tomatoes using a fine cheese grater like the type you'd use for Parmesan. Cup the tomatoes in your fingers or palm so that when you get close to the sharp bit, your fingers are out of the way. You'll be left with a couple of thin layers of tomato skin, discard these.

Finely grate the red onion, adding a little less or more to your taste, followed by the garlic clove. Tip all the grated items into a small bowl, then add the mixed herbs, tomato purée, lime or lemon juice, garlic oil, some black pepper and sugar, if using. Mix well.

Now you can either leave the salsa smooth or finely dice the cherry tomatoes and mix these in too before serving.

pea purée

GF

EF

V

Vg*

DF*

The lemon cuts through the sweetness of the peas here to make a wonderful savoury dip.

350g (2⅔ cups) good-quality frozen peas
50g (¼ cup) cream cheese*

1 tsp garlic paste
juice of 1 small lemon
a few fresh mint leaves, finely

chopped (optional)
a little freshly ground black pepper

Put the frozen peas in a bowl and cover with boiling water out of the kettle. Cover the bowl with a plate and allow to stand for 2–3 minutes until the peas have defrosted.

Meanwhile, add the remaining ingredients to a food processor pot.

Once the peas are defrosted, drain them very well, shaking off any excess water. Add the drained peas to the food processor too, then whizz until the mixture is nice and smooth. Alternatively, you can mash the ingredients together using a potato masher, this will result in a lumpier texture but it is still delicious.

creamy garlic avo dip

Each recipe makes 1 large sharing bowl

Both dips are ready in 5 minutes

Love your leftovers

If you have any leftovers, both these dips will keep in the fridge for up to 2 days. They won't keep well in the freezer.

The avocado adds extra richness to this yogurt dip and mellows out the sourness of the yogurt.

flesh of 1 avocado
½ tsp sesame oil

5 heaped tbsp Greek yogurt*

1 tsp garlic paste
a touch of freshly ground black pepper

GF

EF

V

Vg*

DF*

Mash the avocado flesh with the back of a fork in a bowl. Add the remaining ingredients, mix well and serve.

If you are not planning on eating this straight away, add a good squeeze of lemon juice to stop the avocado from browning.

garlic chive dip

This recipe is a staple in my house, and if you have any of my other books, a version of this dip appears somewhere. I couldn't give you a dip selection without my favourite making an appearance.

5 tbsp thick Greek yogurt*
1 garlic clove, minced
juice of 1 lemon

2 tbsp fresh chives, finely chopped (optional)

a good grinding of black pepper

GF

EF

V

Vg*

DF*

Add all the ingredients to a bowl and mix well to combine before serving.

Both these dips are pictured on page 212.

japanese smacked cucumber pickle

When I eat out at Japanese restaurants, cucumber pickle is always my go-to order. Here is my family-friendly edition, however, adults feel free to add a good dollop of crispy chilli oil or hot sauce to make your portion a little more authentic.

**Serves 2 adults
and 2 littles
as a side**

**Prep 5 minutes,
Rest for at least
10 minutes**

**Love your
leftovers**

This cucumber pickle will keep its crispness for around 24 hours in the fridge, but once it has gone soft, it is no longer good to eat. This dish isn't suitable for freezing.

1 large cucumber,
   washed
1 tbsp apple
   cider vinegar

1 tsp sesame oil
1 tsp minced fresh
   garlic OR 1 tsp garlic
   paste

1 tbsp low-salt
   soy sauce*
2 tbsp sesame seeds,
   preferably toasted

Using a rolling pin or the side of a large knife, firmly smack the cucumber so that it cracks open a little. Rotate the cucumber and hit it around 4–5 times in different positions across the length of the fruit.

Chop the smacked cucumber into large chunks, keeping some pieces in finger-size strips if serving to little ones under 3. Add the cucumber to a medium bowl, along with the rest of the ingredients. Stir well and allow to sit for at least 10 minutes.

Shake off a little of the marinade and serve the cucumber pickle alongside noodle or rice dishes. This is fantastic in a salad or sandwich too.

Switch it up with veggie variations Swap the cucumber for grated or thinly sliced carrots, thinly sliced radishes or finely shredded cabbage.

This recipe is pictured at the bottom of page 196 and on page 39.

picky plates

Here are some quick meal ideas to whip up when you're super short on time, or how about pulling together a few of these to create a bigger platter for a sunny afternoon in the garden. I try to make my picky plates as balanced as possible with a little protein, carbs and plenty of fruit and veg. Don't worry about whether the ingredients really go together – if it's tasty then it goes!

Plate option 1
- Small, sweet snacking peppers, tops cut off, deseeded and halved. I fill these with a little cream cheese and top them with poppy and sesame seeds
- Cucumber sticks
- Crackers

Plate option 2
- Rice cakes topped with peanut butter and mashed banana
- Grated carrot
- Quartered grapes

Plate option 3
- Make your own cracker stackers using small cut-up pieces of ham, slices of cheese and crackers
- Add veg sticks or fruit on the side

Plate option 4
- Bread sticks
- Vegetable crudités
- Dips (see pages 213–214 for dip recipes)

Plate option 5
- Hard-boiled egg, peeled and cut in half
- Toast squares or fingers
- Sugar snap peas
- Grated or sliced cheese
- Chopped fruit

Plate option 6
- Toasted crumpet or bread with sliced cheese on top – pop this in the microwave for 30–60 seconds to melt the cheese
- Veg or fruit sticks on the side

Plate option 7
- My version of peanut butter and jelly sandwiches: replace the jam with very soft sweet fruits like ripe plums or sliced peaches. The juiciness from the fruit cuts through the dryness of the peanut butter
- Serve with extra fruit on the side

10% dairy or fortified alternative (yogurt, cheese and milk as an ingredient for solid foods, in addition to the amount of milk little ones should be having in relation to their age)

25% carbs (such as pasta, rice, potatoes, bread)

40–50% fruit or veg (such as broccoli, carrots, cabbage, apples, berries, cucumber)

25% protein (such as chicken, fish, lentils, chickpeas, tofu)

This chart is a quick reference on how to balance a plate of food. Don't worry if you don't stick to these ratios for every single meal – if you have served less of an element for one meal, just increase this amount for the next one.

banoffee pie toasts

This feels like an utter treat but it's full of healthy ingredients which are transformed into a glorious fuss-free breakfast or dessert.

Makes 2 toasts

Prep and cook 8–10 minutes

Love your leftovers

This dish is best served fresh. The date purée will keep in the fridge for up to 2 days if you have any leftover.

2 thick slices of bread*
3 medjool dates

2 heaped tbsp thick plain yogurt* (extra-thick if possible)

1 banana, peeled and thinly sliced
pinch of ground cinnamon

Boil a kettle with a touch of water at the bottom. Pop the bread in the toaster and toast it to your desired doneness.

Tear the dates into pieces, removing and discarding the stones inside, and place the dates in a small, flat-bottomed bowl. Add 3–4 tablespoons of boiling water from the kettle, then using a fork, mash the dates into a purée. They should break down quite easily.

Once the toast is done, spread half of the date purée over each piece of toast, using a little less if serving to children under 2. Top each piece of toast with a tablespoon of yogurt, spreading it evenly. Finish with sliced bananas on top and a little sprinkle of cinnamon for decoration and flavour.

Adults, the dates and banana make this dish sweet enough, but if you would like an extra sugar kick, drizzle a little honey or maple syrup over the yogurt before topping it with sliced bananas.

Serve as is or cut into finger strips for the little ones – delicious!!

good old-fashioned peach and clementine jelly

A birthday party favourite, also great for a bit of Christmas magic, or even an everyday treat the whole family will love!

Serves 2 adults and 3 littles

Prep 10 minutes, Set 4 hours+

Love your leftovers

Enjoy with cream, ice cream, thick yogurt or just on its own with fruit on the side. This jelly will keep for up to 2–3 days in the fridge, if you have any left!

1 x 415g (15oz) can of peaches in fruit juice

a pinch of ground cinnamon (optional)

6–8 clementines/ satsumas/easy peelers OR 4 oranges

OR 300ml (1¼ cups) shop-bought unsweetened clementine or orange juice (not from concentrate)

1 tsp alcohol-free vanilla extract

1–2 tbsp honey* (for over 1s) or maple syrup (optional)

1 x 12g sachet of gelatine powder* (or ½oz packet of unflavored gelatin*), to make 600ml (2½ cups) of jelly

Add the peaches plus the juice, along with the cinnamon, if using, to a blender and whizz until completely smooth. Alternatively, you can put the ingredients in a large jug and use a stick blender.

Squeeze in the citrus fruit juice to make the quantity of liquid up to just a touch over 600ml (2½ cups) – don't worry about any pulp or pips that may fall in, we'll remove those next.

Pour the fruity juice into another bowl with a fine-mesh sieve set over it to catch any larger pieces of fruit or sneaky pips and make sure the jelly is as smooth as possible. Add the vanilla extract and honey or maple syrup, if using, to the fruit juice and stir well.

Next, add the gelatine powder according to the packet instructions – every version is slightly different so be sure to follow the instructions and adjust the liquid quantity accordingly.

Pour the jelly into moulds or serving bowls and place in the fridge until set; overnight preferably or a minimum of around 4 hours should do the trick.

To remove the jelly from the moulds, fill a deep bowl with hot water and very briefly dip each mould into the hot water, ensuring no water spills over the top and directly touches the jelly. The hot water should melt just the outside of the jelly, allowing it to be released from the mould when it is turned upside down on a serving plate.

Note If you are using a veggie gelatine, the instructions on the packet may require you to heat the liquid, which takes a few extra moments. It will also probably give you a slightly softer set, but equally still very delicious, jelly.

NO COOK

For a firmer jelly
This jelly has a slightly softer-set texture, if you would like a firm jelly, replace the peaches for all fruit juice.

raspberry corn cake yogurt bark

This simple snack is perfect to keep in the freezer for when the little ones want a nibble of something, or for when little baba is teething and needs something cold on their gums. The corn cake provides a little texture and a nice handle to stop those fingers from getting quite so messy – hopefully!

Makes 6 pieces

Prep 5 minutes, Freeze 2 hours+

Freezable

♡

Love your leftovers

These will keep for up to 3 months in the freezer in an airtight container or a sealable freezer bag.

50g (⅓ cup) fresh raspberries
100g (scant ½ cup) full-fat Greek yogurt*

1 tsp alcohol-free vanilla extract
1 tsp maple syrup (optional)

3 large unsweetened and unsalted corn or rice cakes

Add the raspberries to a small bowl and mash them using the back of a fork. Add the yogurt, vanilla extract and maple syrup, if using, then stir well to combine.

Break each corn or rice cake in half so you have 6 roughly half-moon shapes. Hold one corner of a piece of corn or rice cake, then use a spoon to scoop and spread the yogurt mixture over both sides, keeping the corner you are holding clear of yogurt.

Place on a flat tray or a plate that can fit in your freezer, lined with non-stick foil if you're worried about sticking. Repeat with the rest of the corn or rice cakes. Divide any leftover yogurt mixture between the pieces, adding a touch more to the top so there's a nice thick layer of yogurt on each one.

Place the tray or plate in the freezer for a minimum of 2 hours to fully freeze before enjoying at your convenience. After 3 hours, gather any yogurt corn cakes you're saving for later and place them in a sealable freezer bag, this will save you space in the freezer and make them last longer.

Do note that over time, the texture of the corn cakes will change and turn a little softer. They will still be delicious to eat, just a little different from when you first made them.

NO COOK

raspberry, coconut and almond bliss balls

There's something very comforting about a recipe that takes a few minutes to throw together and will keep the kids (and you) happy all week. These super-soft nutty bites do just that. They're a fab pud and perfect as an after-school snack, as part of a picky lunch or for adding to baba's lunchbox for munching on the go.

 GF*

 EF

 V

 Vg

 DF

Makes 14

Prep 5 minutes

Freezable

Love your leftovers

These will keep for up to 1 week in the fridge. Or freeze for up to 1 month in an airtight freezer-safe container. Defrost in the fridge before consuming within 24 hours.

80g (generous 1 cup) desiccated (dried shredded) coconut
50g (½ cup) rolled porridge oats*

100g (1 cup) ground almonds or 100g (¾ cup) coconut flour
70g (¼ cup) almond butter or seed butter

55g (¾ cup) pitted soft dates
80g (⅔ cup) fresh raspberries (or defrosted from frozen)

Reserve roughly 50g (⅔ cup) of the desiccated coconut. Add the rest of the coconut and all the other remaining ingredients to a food processor. Whizz until smooth and the mixture clumps together.

Add the reserved desiccated coconut to a bowl. Take a portion of the mixture, roughly the size of a ping-pong ball, and roll it into a ball between your palms. Drop it into the bowl of coconut and shake the bowl a little until the bliss ball is covered in coconut all over – the tacky texture on the outside means the coconut should stick easily. Transfer the bliss ball to a reusable airtight container and repeat with the remaining mixture.

You will make about 14 bliss balls in total. Serve, or cover tightly and store in the fridge to enjoy later.

chocolate and almond banana sticks

These frozen ice lolly-like treats are super moreish and a great way to incorporate nuts into your diet. You can swap the almond butter for smooth peanut butter if preferred, just make sure that you always buy 100% nut butter with no added ingredients.

Makes 4 sticks

40g (2½ tbsp) almond butter, plus extra to decorate

70g (¼ cup) thick full-fat Greek yogurt*

2 tsp unsweetened cocoa powder

1 tsp maple syrup (optional)

1 large ripe banana

1 tsp unsweetened desiccated (dried shredded) coconut (optional)

Prep 7 minutes, Freezing time 3 hours+

Add half of the almond butter, the yogurt, cocoa powder and maple syrup, if using, to a bowl and mix well.

Peel the banana and cut it into 1cm (½in) thick rounds. Skewer a lolly stick through the centre of one banana round, then spread a little bit of the remaining almond butter on the top of the banana. Add a second piece of banana and push it down so that the stick just pokes through the other side. Add more almond butter to this banana piece, then finally thread one last piece of banana onto the lolly stick.

Freezable

Using the back of a spoon, coat the outside of the banana lolly with a quarter of the cocoa yogurt mixture, then place the lolly on a tray lined with non-stick baking paper. Repeat the process to make 4 lollies in total, then sprinkle over the desiccated coconut, if using, and a touch more almond butter for a little decoration. Pop the tray in the freezer for a minimum of 3 hours, or until frozen solid before enjoying.

♡

Love your leftovers

These will keep in the freezer for up to 3 months.

Once frozen solid, you can gather the sticks and store them in an airtight container in the freezer, if you wish.

cherry and mango frozen yogurt

Whether you're after a quick treat on a warm day or one that can be prepped ahead of time, this creamy fro-yo will be your go-to. Soft, melty and sweet with no added sugar, it's perfect for all the family.

 GF

 EF

 V

 Vg*

 DF*

Makes approx. 700ml (3 cups) of frozen yogurt

Prep 4 minutes

Freezable

Love your leftovers

This will store in the freezer for up to 3 months. Allow it to stand at room temperature for 30 minutes or until soft enough to scoop with a hot ice-cream scoop or a spoon dipped in boiling water.

5 small soft dates, pitted (optional)
200g (1 cup) thick full-fat Greek yogurt*

300g (10½oz) frozen mango chunks, unsweetened
2 tsp alcohol-free vanilla extract

300g (10½oz) frozen pitted cherries, unsweetened

If using the dates, add them to a food processor along with the yogurt and blend for 20 seconds. Add the remaining ingredients (or add all the ingredients with the yogurt in one go if you aren't using dates) and whizz for 2–3 minutes until super smooth with no lumps of fruit left.

Either serve straight away as a soft-serve style ice cream, or immediately pour into an airtight lidded container and freeze to have another day. If you plan to freeze it, don't allow the mixture to defrost before freezing as it will become solid rather than creamy.

Serve in bowls or in cones, with some crushed nuts, grated chocolate (for bigger kids) or pieces of fruit on top, if you wish.

peanut butter and chocolate puffed rice cakes

A healthier take on the age-old favourite puffed rice cereal treats. This version swaps the sugary marshmallows for nutrient-dense peanut butter. Technically, you'll have to use the microwave for this one to melt the ingredients at the start, but that's all the 'cooking' there is – promise!

 GF*

 EF

 V

 Vg*

 DF*

Makes 8 cakes

60g (¼ cup) unsalted butter*
90g (scant ½ cup smooth peanut butter (100% nuts)

40g (⅛ cup) honey* (for babies under 1, see note)
3 heaped tsp unsweetened cocoa powder

80g (3⅓ cups) unsweetened puffed rice cereal* (this can be swapped for cornflakes too)

Prep 10 minutes, Chill/freeze 20–60 minutes

Find 8, preferably non-stick, paper muffin cases and have them ready to one side.

Add the butter, peanut butter and honey (or alternative, see note), to a medium-sized bowl and pop in the microwave on LOW for 1–2 minutes until melted.

Love your leftovers

Once the cakes are set, store them in the fridge for up to 3–4 days, but do note the cereal may turn a little stale over time.

Stir well, then add the cocoa powder and stir again. Pour in the puffed rice cereal and stir to coat it in the melted butter mixture before dividing between the 8 paper cases.

Place the cakes in the fridge for at least 1 hour until set. You can speed this process up by popping the cakes in the freezer for 20–30 minutes.

Note It is important to avoid serving honey to babies under the age of 1, as there is a high risk of infant botulism, which can cause serious illness. Instead, swap the honey for golden (corn) syrup or light soft brown sugar. For babies under 1, it's also important to keep the added sugar to a minimum, so I recommend halving the quantity or removing the sugar or syrup altogether. Do note, the reduction of sugar in this recipe will result in a softer set and the puffed rice may not stick together fully, therefore, I recommend freezing (rather than chilling in the fridge) to help give the cakes a stronger set.

conversions

If required, we recommend you follow the conversions as listed on the individual recipes, however, here is a handy list of standard conversions should you need them for anything else.

Dry measures

15g	½oz
30g	1oz
60g	2oz
90g	3oz
125g	4oz (¼lb)
155g	5oz
185g	6oz
220g	7oz
250g	8oz (½lb)
280g	9oz
315g	10oz
345g	11oz
375g	12oz (¾lb)
410g	13oz
440g	14oz
470g	15oz
500g	16oz (1lb)
750g	24oz (1½lb)
1kg	32oz (2lb)

Length measures

3mm	⅛in
6mm	¼in
1cm	½in
2cm	¾in
2.5cm	1in
5cm	2in
6cm	2½in
8cm	3in
10cm	4in
13cm	5in
15cm	6in
18cm	7in
20cm	8in
22cm	9in
25cm	10in
28cm	11in
30cm	12in (1ft)

Australia – UK spoon measures

½ tbsp	2 tsp
1 tbsp	1 heaped tbsp
2 tbsp (8 tsp)	2½ tbsp
3 tbsp (12 tsp)	4 tbsp
4 tbsp (16 tsp)	5 tbsp
5 tbsp (20 tsp)	6½ tbsp
6 tbsp (24 tsp)	8 tbsp

Volume measures

75ml	2½fl oz
90ml	3fl oz
100ml	3½fl oz
120ml	4fl oz
150ml	5fl oz
200ml	7fl oz
240ml	8fl oz
250ml	9fl oz
300ml	10fl oz
350ml	12fl oz
400ml	14fl oz
450ml	15fl oz
500ml	16fl oz
600ml	1 pint
750ml	1¼ pints
900ml	1½ pints
1 litre	1¾ pints
1.2 litres	2 pints
1.4 litres	2½ pints
1.5 litres	2¾ pints
1.7 litres	3 pints
2 litres	3½ pints
3 litres	5¼ pints

Oven temperatures

130°C	110°C fan /250°F /Gas ½
140°C	120°C fan /275°F /Gas 1
150°C	130°C fan /300°F /Gas 2
160°C	140°C fan /325°F /Gas 3
180°C	160°C fan /350°F /Gas 4
190°C	170°C fan /375°F /Gas 5
200°C	180°C fan /400°F /Gas 6
220°C	200°C fan /425°F /Gas 7
230°C	210°C fan /455°F /Gas 8
240°C	220°C fan /475°F /Gas 9

index

acknowledgments

Thank you to all my friends and family, to Nina and her daddy and all of my extended family, but especially my dear pal Joanna for your continued support on this cookery journey of mine – you're there through my ups and downs and for that I'm forever grateful.

My literary agent Darryl, you are so much more than an agent to me now, you're a true friend and I'm blessed to have your kindness and support in my life. None of this would be possible without your guidance – thank you.

To all the team at DK, from editorial and production to sales and marketing, thank you for supporting me every step of the way. This book marks my fourth cookbook, but also my fourth and final book produced with my lovely editor Steph, who is moving on from DK to pastures new. Thank you for believing in me right at the beginning – it has been amazing working with you.

Alice, Amy and Kiron, you have been the backbone of helping to create this book, you listen to all of my requests and have worked so hard to make this book as amazing as it is! Your efficiency is extremely appreciated, thank you. And Lucy, thank you once again for casting your expert nutritionist eye over the book.

Bess, you're a wonderful, kind person and I have thoroughly enjoyed working with you on the photoshoots for this book. Doing something you love makes work feel less like "work", but even more so when you get to do it with people who make you smile. Not to mention, your art direction is so invaluable – you've made the imagery for this book look incredible, thank you!

Clare, you're kind, funny, patient, talented, understanding and efficient, not to mention you take such stunning photographs. It's a joy to work with you. Danielle, thank you for your gorgeous portrait photography, especially of my Nina – these are memories I will cherish.

Maud and Flossy, I just love working with you both. So quick, so efficient, you make the food look amazing and are so understanding of my specific directions. It's simply a joy to have you on the shoots.

Thank you to Kidly, Les Petits Essentiels and Bamboo Bamboo for kindly supplying your wonderful products for our photoshoots.

And finally, to all who follow along on my social media and buy my books, if you are holding this book and reading it for yourself right now, I thank you dearly for being here. My goal is to try and help as many families as I can by taking the stress out of cooking, and that will always be my number one priority, but it would be dishonest to avoid mentioning that I dearly love this process and I am very proud to say that this is my job. So thank you for allowing all this to happen.

about the author

Rebecca Wilson is a mum to her 4-year-old daughter Nina, a recipe developer, and founder of her own food channel *Rebecca Wilson*. Her mission is to make family mealtimes easy for everyone and to show parents and carers that introducing solid foods can be fun, exciting, easy, and most importantly... delicious!

She creates recipes for the whole family, so that babies reaching their weaning milestone at six months old can eat the same meal together with their older siblings – and even the adults too! The best benefit is that you only need to cook one meal to feed the whole gang. You can find Rebecca over on her Instagram channel @*rebeccawilsonfood* where she shares quick and easy meal ideas that are suitable for all the family to enjoy together.

Rebecca's first book, *What Mummy Makes,* published in July 2020 to immediate acclaim and quickly became a chart and *Sunday Times* No. 1 bestseller. It won the Wordery Food & Drink Book of the Year 2020 and was shortlisted for the 2021 British Book Awards Book of the Year in Non-fiction Lifestyle. Rebecca has gone on to publish two more bestselling cookery books: *What Mummy Makes Family Meal Planner* and *Family Comforts*. This is her fourth book.

To find out more head to **www.rebeccawilson.com** and **@rebeccawilsonfood** on Instagram.

Also available by Rebecca Wilson:

Publishing Director Katie Cowan
Art Director Maxine Pedliham
Senior Acquisitions Editor Stephanie Milner
Project Editor Kiron Gill
Designer Amy Cox
DTP Designer Anurag Trivedi
Jackets Coordinator Jasmin Lennie
Senior Production Editor Tony Phipps
Senior Production Controller Stephanie McConnell

Photography Direction Bess Daly
Editor Alice Sambrook
Dietary Consultant Lucy Upton
Proofreader Anne Sheasby
Indexer Vanessa Bird
Prop Stylist Polly Webb-Wilson
Food Stylists Maud Eden, Flossy McAslan
Hair and Makeup Victoria Barnes
Author portrait photography by Danielle Wood
Recipe photography by Clare Winfield

First published in Great Britain in 2022 by
Dorling Kindersley Limited
DK, One Embassy Gardens, 8 Viaduct Gardens,
London, SW11 7BW

The authorised representative in the EEA is
Dorling Kindersley Verlag GmbH.
Arnulfstr. 124, 80636 Munich, Germany

Text copyright © 2022 Rebecca Wilson
Rebecca Wilson has asserted her right to
be identified as the author of this work.

Copyright © 2022 Dorling Kindersley Limited
A Penguin Random House Company
10 9 8 7 6 5 4 3 2 1
001–326619–Sep/2022

A CIP catalogue record for this book
is available from the British Library.
ISBN: 978-0-2415-3470-0

Printed in China

For the curious
www.dk.com

This book was made with Forest Stewardship
Council ™ certified paper - one small step in
DK's commitment to a sustainable future.
For more information go to
www.dk.com/our-green-pledge

FOOD NOTES

Recipes have been developed using
a 950W microwave – please adjust
the timings slightly if the power of
your microwave is any different.

All-rounder potatoes are equivalent
to all-purpose varieties in the US –
Yukon Gold is a good example.

Egg sizes given in recipes are UK.
US sizes are as follows:

UK medium = US large

UK large = US extra-large

DISCLAIMER

Those following strict allergen
diets should always check
the packet for guidance
about suitability.

The advice given in this book
is based on the UK national
health system guidance for
family eating and baby
weaning, therefore if you live
outside of the UK and are ever
in doubt, refer to your own
country's guidance for
new parents.